IRAN: FROM CALIPHS TO ISLAMIC REPUBLIC

Iran: From Caliphs to Islamic Republic

by

Farokh Yazdani

Published by CreateSpace

ISBN-13: 978-1522852766
ISBN-10: 152285276X

Contents

Introduction

When somebody asks me, "Where are you from?" I always need to think, *Should I call it Persia or Iran?* For five thousand years, the country's name was Persia. Seventy-five years ago, it was changed to Iran. But I will proudly call it Persia, as it has been a center of science and civilization and a country associated with the world's oldest culture that has greatly contributed to the world for centuries. Many great kings have left their legacies by pushing the country forward, building the foundation of a better life for the future world.

All those kings had one thing in common— they followed the teaching of Zartosht, the oldest prophet, who lived around 2500 BC. He was born in a province of Azerbaijan in the north of Persia. For thousands of years, this was the state religion of Persia. This changed in AD 634, when Persia was overrun by a bunch of barbarians under the orders of Caliph Omar. They were ruthless tribesmen who invaded the country with the purpose of introducing a new religion. It started with masked horsemen who cut off heads with their swords, heads that rolled in rivers of blood. Cities and villages, one after the other, were set on fire. This was initiated by Ayesha (the Islamic prophet's wife) and continued by Caliph Omar in Medina. The caliphs ruled over Persia for 624 years until 1258, when the Mongols invaded the country. During this period, Syria, Iraq, and Persia were ruled by caliphs from Baghdad. The Persians accepted the new religion, Islam, under pressure, although it was not the one that was introduced by Arabs. They made their own version of Islam, Shiite, as opposed to Sunni Islam, which was led by the caliphs.

In this book, I will discuss the history of Persia before and after the rule of the caliphs. For thousands of years, Persia was ruled by many dynasties. It was a great, free country. Its citizens lived side by side with the rest of the world, minding their own business, enjoying their lives. They were living in peace and harmony with the rest of world. From China to Europe, as far as they could reach, they traded their goods and culture. They respected each other's religions and traditions. Like America now, Persia was a superpower and the envy of the world. This all ended when the caliphs took over and made life a living hell for Persia's citizens. Fourteen centuries passed, the world moved into the twenty-first century, but Persia has remained in the dark ages since the introduction of Islam. There was just a short period of fifty years during the Pahlavi dynasty that is known as the golden age of Persia. In this short period of time, Persia, now called Iran, had the freedom and opportunity to act and bring the country in line with the rest of the developed world. This shows that when Persia has the opportunity, it will shine and its people will show their intellect and talents. Sadly, this golden age ended in 1979 when mullahs took over and pushed Persia back into a time when the caliphs were ruling.

Persian Religion before Islam

When most of the world were worshiping objects as gods, the Persians believed in one god—Ahuramazda, the only god, who created the universe, the earth, and all the creatures on earth. Zartosht, the founder of this religion, asked his followers to adopt the religion so they would be protected by Ahuramazda, their god. His beliefs were built on the ideas of "good thought," "good words," and "good deeds." Life built upon these three pillars would bear the fruits of success, resulting in an easy, happy life. The other option was to go the path of Ahriman, who was evil and guided his victims onto the path of darkness.

Lying is the greatest sin in Zoroastrianism. To avoid it, most citizens chose farming over other occupations that might occasionally require them to not tell the truth. Kourosh (Cyrus the Great), the writer of the first human-rights charter, was a devout Zoroastrian. In 535 BC when he conquered Babylon, he freed thousands of Hebrews from exile so that they could go home to Jerusalem and freely worship their god, Yahweh, who is aligned with Ahuramazda. Many Zoroastrian kings before and after him conquered new lands and expanded their territories for the benefit of their own citizens and the conquered populations, both from a moral perspective and for economic purposes, improving the standards of living and contributing to their well-being and sharing their advanced knowledge. Persian kings never disrespected others' beliefs or forced the conquered citizens to accept the religion of their conquerors.

A Zoroastrian place of worship is called *Darb-e-Mehr* ("door to kindness"). There is another name for it, "house of permanent fire," as a fire is kept at the center of the building under the dome with two tall chimneys on each side, which is visible from a distance. To pray, a

Zartoshti (another name for a Zoroastrian) has to face the light: daytime toward the sun and after dark, candles or fire. In Darb-e-Mehr, those who pray face toward the permanent fire. A caretaker watches the fire, 24-7; its extinguishing would be like a modern-day power outage. It is the source of fire for citizens to ignite their candles or the wood in their kitchen for cooking.

Right now, the population of Iran is about seventy-seven million. From that, only fifty thousand are Zartoshti. They survived the harsh climate of discrimination, and they are considered inferior in many ways to Muslims, although they are in their own homeland.

The Birth of Islam

Prophet Mohammad was born in AD 570 in a leading Arab tribe, the Quraysh, in Mecca. He married a wealthy widow named Khadijah, who had a caravan of camels with which to trade goods in the surrounding area. She was losing the fight against raids on her caravan on the trade routes. Therefore, she hired Mohammad to watch and protect her caravans from attackers. Although she was fifteen years older than Mohammad was, she married him some time later. She was the one who witnessed the angel Gabriel coming to Mohammad in his sleep. On that historic night that is now known as "the night of Qadr" in the month of Ramadan in the year of AD 610, the revelation came through an angel who said that his name was Gabriel and that he came from Allah. The angel forced Mohammad to accept the words of Allah and to be Allah's messenger. When Khadijah shared this incident with her uncle, a Christian, he assured her that Mohammad was the chosen one and she should accept this and believe him. She did, so she received the honor to be the first Muslim in history. Nine years later, she died at the age of sixty-four. She left behind four daughters from her marriage with Mohammad.

Mohammad had difficulty in convincing the Arabs—who had no religion—and especially his tribe, that he was the chosen one. Three years after Khadijah's death in 622, he moved to an oasis near Medina named Umma of Medina, where three Jewish tribes and a few Arab tribes were living side by side. A group of men, an opposition from Mecca, followed him everywhere. They made life difficult for him, as they didn't trust him. They did not believe his words were from god because of his background and the people he had been in contact with. At some point, he was broke and without any hope. He had no other option but to turn to the practice of *ghazu* (raids on caravans travelling the trade routes). From that, he gained wealth and prestige, and then he moved to Medina. A year later, he led an army of three hundred and fifty men to the well of Badr to raid the largest Meccan caravan. His successful strategy was to take advantage of water wells, where the caravans were most vulnerable. The real war between him and his own tribe began when he sent a few of his men to kill and silence those who had been obstacles and opposition to him. In 626, when a large army of Quraysh marched to Medina to get rid of Mohammad for good, he pulled a trick he had learned from Salman-e-Pars, a priest who had escaped the execution from the then king of Persia. He built a trench along a high wall of dirt. While the Quraysh army stared at the trench in bewilderment, a shower of arrows came from behind the wall. They realized they were sitting ducks and hastily withdrew until they were out of range. This victory opened the way for him to go back to Mecca and sign a treaty with the Quraysh that said that he and his followers would be free to travel back and forth between Mecca and Medina.

Ayesha

Mohammad's third wife (out of seven), Ayesha, was nine years old when he married her, and at the age of eighteen, she was a widow. For her age, she was an ambitious, clever girl. Mohammad trusted her to be in charge of the religious movement and its expansion. She chose and supported future caliphs to rule Sunni Muslims and form an opposition against Shiite imams. She had a vision to promote an independent Arabic religion for Arabs only. There were no rules among the Arabs other than the rules of the jungle. The secret to survival was to get involved in tribal fights and steal from each other. Live domestic animals, especially camels, were among the most popular items that the thieves were after. The robberies happened mostly in the darkness of the night. Only a dog was an effective tool to watch and protect the most valuable possessions the people had. This made man's best friend unpopular with Muslims. Now dogs are negatively associated with the Muslim faith throughout the world.

Caliphate

The first caliph after Mohammad's death in AD 632 was his closest friend, Abu Bakr, who had received the assignment from Mohammad to continue the movement after his death. He was the father of Mohammad's wife Ayesha.

From the beginning, it proved to be a difficult task for Abu Bakr to keep together the group of followers who had been members of Mohammad's circle in a time of peace and war. After his death, they thought their commitment and dues had been directly to him and that these would end at his death. They had benefited from the attacks on the caravans and had paid membership in a way similar to the modern Mafia. It was more convenient for them to go back to their traditional ways of living, the life they knew and had been accustomed to. It was of no interest or benefit for them to continue to follow and pay a percentage of their income (*zakat*), similar to an income tax, to

Caliph Abu Bakr. This trend continued with no solution in sight until Abu Bakr made it into law that "punishment for breaking the commitment and leaving the group is death." This law stopped the trend, but it created an obstacle to recruiting additional members. Finally, after two years of struggle and health problems, on the advice of Mohammad's wife Ayesha, Abu Bakr gave up the effort, and she put another man, Omar, in charge. Below we will see what this aggressive, radical, and inhuman person did to Persia.

Abu Bakr died two years later at the age of sixty-three, and he was buried next to Mohammad in Medina in Saudi Arabia.

Caliph Omar

As far as Persia was concerned, choosing Omar as caliph was the worst possible choice Ayesha could have made. Omar and Abu Bakr had been constant companions of Mohammad, but Omar, with his aggressive behavior, was not Mohammad's favorite person to be a caliph. It was the beginning of the end of civilization and of life as the Persians knew it. Omar's actions had long-lasting consequence and left a mark on the world, especially Persia. Nobody knew about oil then, but Persia (Iran), the ultimate source of wealth, was located next door to the poorest desert dwellings. Omar had neither an army nor knowledge to train one with. He began to unite the Arabic-speaking tribes around the Arabian Peninsula. His message was to stop the fighting among themselves and unite, so that all effort was given to create easier and larger rewards in this life and beyond. He kept sending low-life, hopeless men armed with swords and riding on horses toward Persia where the people were living, working, and prospering with plentiful, God-given resources like fertile land and water. The mission of Omar's men was to terrorize, kill, rape, and steal from the defenseless, innocent peasants in their fields, homes, and places of worship. Like a pack of wolves, attacks continued, wave after wave, in unpredictable places, leaving behind widespread death and destruction. Omar took advantage of the young and inexperienced Persian king who had been crowned a short time before. Omar knew more about Persia than King Yazdegerd himself did. For years in Mecca, Omar had been the companion of Salman-e-Pars, who had been one of the king's ministers but had turned out to be the king's archenemy due to the constant disagreements between the two.

King Yazdegerd was powerless, and he did not know the reason for the actions of the Arabs. He sent a message to Omar and asked for an explanation for their barbarous acts. Omar in turn sent fourteen men to talk with the king. When the king asked the messengers the reason for their aggressive behavior toward his empire, one of the fourteen replied, "Allah commanded us, by the mouth of his prophet, to extend the dominion of Islam over all nations."

The king told them, "I and my people are happy with what we have. What more do you have to offer?" They left giving no answer, and instead Omar intensified his daily raids on innocent Persian populations. This continued until the king declared war against the invaders and sent an army led by the Persian officer Bahman to stop and punish them. This resulted in a victory for the king and a great loss and setback for the invaders. However, this didn't stop Omar; he continued terrorizing the country from every direction. This was not the way to spread the word of Allah. He was taking advantage of a young and inexperienced king, by killing harmless, defenseless civilian women and children.

King Yazdegerd went on the offense to keep the Arabs out. He sent his army all over the place to put stop to this group of ruthless terrorists who were using hit-and-run tactics, and who had no fear of death since they had been promised that they would go to heaven. The attacks continued against harmless, terrified citizens, mostly farmers, who were no match for those vicious, brutal, killing machines. Their only option was to run out of the invaders' way, hiding in the mountains and caves, hoping this would pass soon.

The attackers progressed deeper into the land of honey and beautiful women, meeting little or no resistance. They bribed local traitors with land, cattle, and livelihood taken from those who were killed when resisting or those who had run away. All this happened under watch of Ayesha, the architect of all these mishaps. She continued to support and encourage Omar to commit these barbarous acts.

The ball of Islam started to roll when Khadijah, Mohammad's first wife, saw the angel Gabriel talking to Mohammad in his sleep, and Ayesha, his other wife, kept the ball rolling through the blood of Persians until it became a religion. The irony is this religion is now spread all over the world, and women are considered as half a person in every aspect of life. They are discriminated against, kept in the shadows, and stripped of the rights and privileges that the rest of the world's females enjoy.

There was no end in sight. Omar had promised his men that if they died, a martyr's reward of seventy-two virgins awaited each of them in paradise. This intensified their destructive actions, while there was little or no resistance.

The people in trouble had lost hope of receiving help from their king. They would have done anything to survive. Resistance fighting aggravated the enemy by intensifying the revenge of burning cities and villages to the ground and killing the fighters with torture, cutting piece-by-piece parts of his body until he died.

The mountain roads and long passes contributed to the lack of communication between the king and those in trouble, and it was another obstacle for the king to act against the terrorists. Because this had never happened throughout history, authorities at the beginning didn't take the violence seriously. It was considered a temporary and isolated act.

The inexperienced king could not even maintain control over his administration, which caused fighting and chaos within his council of ministers.

The king's army was trained to fight conventional wars and did not know how to handle unorganized hit-and-run attacks by a bunch of wild men who terrorized unarmed civilians with gruesome acts of violence.

Arabs kept coming on horses and camels and by foot to take a piece of the pie. Like a fast-moving tsunami, it continued in every direction. Nothing and nobody was safe in the attackers' path. The young and inexperienced king lost hope. Therefore, he handed the crown and the responsibility to his close relative, Farrokhzad. The new king gathered and reorganized Persian resistance fighters to continue their battles against the invaders. Eventually, he too realized that it would be suicidal to continue. Therefore, he gave up the effort and followed the path of the king. The former king had taken his treasury along with some of his servants from the capital city of Ctesiphon toward the remote mountains in the center of Persia.

Not long after, this place of refuge became their final resting place. He and his family died from hunger but with dignity and not at the hand of the enemy. Their resting place has become a popular shrine. Once a year, Zoroastrians from all over the world gather at this isolated mountain. Life-supporting water drips like rain from the ceiling of a solid rock into a pond below in a corner of the mountain all year round.

From King Yazdegerd's family, his daughter Shahrbanu was captured, and together with other females, delivered to Medina. On her arrival, she was introduced to Omar as a Persian princess. It was expected she would get special treatment. Omar had no interest in her and didn't care for her past. Instead, he auctioned her to the highest bidder. Ali, the cousin and son-in-law of Mohammad, was among the highest bidders. He delivered Shahrbanu as a Persian souvenir to his son Hussein.

Their barbaric acts continued until Omar and Ayesha concluded that they had been dealing with a king who was no more than a paper tiger. Now they had a free ride, which encouraged them to intensify their actions. There was nothing in the way to stop them. Looting was the main activity, with Omar in Medina waiting anxiously to receive his share. After some delay, he lost his patience and wrote the following in a letter to his deputy, Amr ibn al-As, who was in charge of gathering the loot: "I have not heard from you. I am very worried. You know I have put my trust in your hand. Please let me know when the goods are going to arrive."

Amr ibn al-As replied, "I have been loyal to you and will continue to serve you. The longest caravan with loot is on its way." To describe the magnitude of the loot, he wrote, "You will see the head of the caravan in Medina and me at the end of the caravan back here."

It is obvious that it had never been Omar's intention to introduce a religion, because no religion is spread by killing, raping, and stealing. On the other hand, Islam would never be a religion if Omar had not attacked Persia. This provided all the fuel it needed to go forward. That was only the beginning of the process of soaking up the entire wealth of Persia and moving it to Medina. As time passed, more and more Arabs, like hungry wolves, made their way into the dead, defenseless country once called Persia.

As the wealth moved west into the Arabian Peninsula, so too did the demand grow for Persian women. The newly rich Arabs developed a taste for beautiful Persian women. They became an important, profitable, hot commodity. Ayesha not only did not condemn this. To the contrary, she considered this act as a reward for her men. This was only part of their inhuman activities. They continued mass killing innocent citizens, raping women and children, and stealing the little food their victims had and letting them starve. To protect females, especially young girls, and keep them out of reach of these strangers, the Persians converted an underground barn into a group hiding resort. The Arabs went door to door to find their victims. It was common to torture a citizen into revealing the hiding places of the females.

Dakhma

As mentioned, Omar never intended to introduce a religion to Persia, nor did he have a religious book to back it up. In ten years of his caliphate, he robbed the people's wealth, pride, and dignity, and in the end, he broke their spirits. He degraded them as subhumans. This started with humiliating and insulting Zoroastrian priests (*dastur*), burning libraries and religious books, and then calling them *gabr* (fire worshiper).

When there is no respect for human life, of course there is no dignity for the dead body. To get rid of corpses and unclaimed human bodies from the trenches and roadsides, killers dragged the bodies behind their horses away from the populated areas to higher ground, leaving them for hyenas and vultures to consume. This continued for years until it became the way of getting rid of human corpses. With time, this action replaced the traditional burying procedure. It started with Omar's caliphate in 634 and continued with other caliphs after him.

Even at the present time, fourteen centuries later, Zoroastrians use a structure built on the mountain or hilltop. This place is call *dakhma*. The corpse of the deceased will be carried there and left for the vultures to consume. Travelling around Yazd and Kerman, many of such structures are visible from the roadside. If one doesn't know the history, one might think the structures are water reservoirs. Men in white coveralls carry the corpses along the zigzag road up to the dakhma. There, at the foot of a high wall, they push to move a heavy stone, which covers a three-by-three-foot opening, to the inside. The rule is that only one of the corpse bearers is allowed to go through to the other side and pull the corpse in. He then carefully lays it on a flat stone at the center. As soon as he leaves, the vultures descend from the high wall for an easy meal. The corpse bearer is not allowed to disclose what he has seen inside. The bones and remains will slide down the mountain slope and pile up against the wall below.

With time, stories have developed about these places. It has been said that vultures always take the right eye first. Or, if somebody has been sinful, the vultures will reject the body and leave it untouched. The corpse bearers are not allowed to come into contact with anybody until they finish the job, take a shower, and change their clothing. Zoroastrian refugees to India continue to practice this kind of funeral there too; they call the place Tower of Silence. This has become a tourist attraction in India.

Zoroastrians believe that at certain times of the year, the souls of their ancestors will come back to earth for a visit. On this day, Zoroastrians gather at the foot of a dakhma. They carry with them whatever their loved one liked the most in his or her lifetime—usually fruit, sweets, and wine. The offerings are neatly placed in front of the gate of the dakhma. Down below, they will celebrate all day with music and dance. This will satisfy the souls of the ancestors and make sure that life continues with happiness.

Shirin

Bahram and his family were average people; he was a hardworking peasant who lived with his wife and nine-year-old daughter in a small village where everybody knew each other. Like everyone else, he was working hard to provide for his family. Recently, a dark cloud of fear and anger hung above the family's heads and made their lives a living hell.

One day, the sound of a stranger's footsteps was heard along the mud-built tunnel leading to his house. It drove a shivering fear through the family's hearts and spines. It sounded like a giant rattlesnake was crawling to their den to swallow them alive.

Three Arab men came to take their only child—their nine-year-old daughter, Shirin, who was pulled out from the hiding hole made for this purpose on the floor of the kitchen and covered with dry bush used for fire.

She struggled and attempted to free herself with her nails and teeth from under the arm of a scary, dangerous masked man. Bahram and his wife were, meanwhile, busy fighting the other two men. It was as if hell had broken loose—a lot of shouting, pulling, and pushing—the neighbors and others joining them to help to free Shirin. She was a sweet, loving girl. Taking her away would break everybody's hearts. It was unthinkable for Bahram and his wife to continue to live without her. The struggle continued until Bahram's senseless, motionless body lay on the floor. He had been kicked in the head by one of the masked man while he had been down. To him, the world suddenly darkened, and the attacker left him for dead. His wife's attention turned to her daughter, who was calling and crying for help. She chose to leave her seemingly dead husband and ran to catch up with her daughter. She gave up the fight and start begging the men to take her along with her daughter.

In the *caravanserai* (house of caravan), the two clenched together, waiting for their dark destiny. To their comfort, they saw others with the same fate in different sections, bundled and ready for delivery. The caravan of women followed the same highway that was used to deliver treasures out of Persia.

Hours passed until Bahram woke up to realize what had happened. He began yelling, calling his wife and daughter. He had no eyes to see or any working muscles and bones in his body to move. His old neighbor, a widow who was taking care of him, gave him the bad news. Against her advice, he left home as soon as he was able to walk and follow the footsteps of his family. He didn't get too far to run out of water and food, but he had no other option than to continue or die. On the road, he saw his fate, walking on the remains of others who tried before him. He never came back home, but his wife did. She had been left behind when, early one morning, she woke up to notice her

33

daughter's caravan with other young girls had quietly left. Nobody knew where, maybe Mecca, Medina, or some other place. She lost track of her daughter and had no other option than to go back home with a broken heart. She arrived to see the empty nest. Up to the day she died, she was hoping that one day she would hear the sound of Shirin's footsteps walking to her and that she'd be able to hug her again.

Transporting Persian Females

It was a delicate task to deliver these females on camels through the harsh Arabian Desert. The weak and lucky ones didn't make it through the journey; the rest lost their freshness, color, and beauty. To deliver this merchandise in better shape, it was necessary to protect it from the elements, like sun, wind, and dust. This problem was solved by covering them up. To that purpose, an individual tent (*chador*) was invented.

From then on, they would be herded to the market in a chador. Only serious buyers were allowed to peek under the chador before making their choices. When more women continued to arrive, the market started to saturate, and the Arabs demanded younger, newer girls who were virgins. This opened the gate for children as low as six years to enter the market.

There was no limit to how many of them a man could take home. Some took more than they could care for or feed. To support their owners, those girls became sex slaves, and they were leased to others for a period, sometimes as little as one hour, a day, or longer. In Arabic, the word for this practice is *sighah* ("temporary marriage").

Walking through town, the woman had to walk a certain distance behind her new master to avoid him being embarrassed by the merchant and others. Any baby girl born from such a woman was subjected to death. The man who fathered it would carry it to an open trench and bury it alive. It is hard to believe that such a thing could ever happen! Out of necessity, the following temporary rules and regulation were created. They later became the basis of sharia law:

- The legal age of consent for a girl was set at nine.

- Killing a newborn child was forbidden.

The following special rules were made for captured Persian women, rules that continue to the present time:

- Men can marry and divorce the captured woman at any time.

- The captured woman has no right to inheritance.

- Her individual chador (head cover), called *hijab-e-Islami* (Islamic head cover), became a very important part of the religion.

- Without her man's permission, she is not allowed to travel or even leave the house.

- The law forbids women to be sex slaves. However, they can still be rented to others legally with a temporary marriage called sighah.

In Iran, sighah has become an alternative to marriage for young males who cannot afford to form a family. Soon after the Islamic revolution in 1979, the legal brothels that were regulated with weekly visits to doctors and a legal permit were demolished, and mobs set many of the girls working there on fire, carrying their charred bodies through the street as a lesson for future females not to practice this kind of occupation.

Now every corner of every street has legally become a brothel, where girls wearing hijab-e-Islami look for customers, who stop their cars and take a quick look to discover what is under the chador.

Another legal option for single men to satisfy their sexual demands is to look for a divorcee or widow, especially after the eight-year war with Iraq, when millions of young men perished and left their wives and children behind. The government promotes this activity for supporting families with no income. A woman can advertise herself for sighah. She will leave her picture, physical description, age, and personality in a mullah's album that can be found in any section of the mosque or at his own advertised place of business. It is obvious that the mullah will keep the young and good-looking ones for himself and under his own protection. He will charge a finder's fee and a fee to register the marriage in his book. After reading some Arabic sentences, he declares the couple *halal* to each other as husband and wife. If the groom already has a wife and family, he will share the time and pays the rent and other living expenses for her as long as the contract lasts. The contract can be renewed for a certain period, and that only costs a visit to the mullah's shop. In this business, they are obligated to hold to the end of the contract, even if he leaves her. Legally, he is the father of any child made by him during this period. This service is only available to men. As far as the young girl goes, she has to protect her virginity until somebody comes along to marry her permanently. The longer she waits, the greater chance she has to become a second or third wife to a rich man. In other Muslim countries, women willing to sighah hang around hotel lobbies. Future grooms will talk directly to them. After they come to an agreement, instead of the mullah, the clerk at the front desk will register their temporary marriage.

In Islam, by law a man can marry up to four women. However, like any other law, a paragraph is attached to it—"Wealthy men have no limit on the number of women they can marry as long they are able to provide for them."

To accommodate the large number of wives under one roof, the house of a harem was built. Only one man other than the master is allowed to live and mingle with the women in the harem. He is a eunuch: a castrated man whose testicles have been brutally damaged in infancy. As a result, he can never become a real man. Hair does not grow on his face; his voice remains as high as an immature boy. His job is to look over his master's wives like a shepherd dog, inside and outside the harem, where they walk like a group of penguins. He makes sure nobody touches or talks to them.

He does the shopping, and he is an entertainer too. Usually a poor family with many children will sacrifice one of their sons to become a eunuch. He is like the premium on an insurance policy, the beneficiaries of which are his parents. This guarantees the well-being of the whole family.

In Islam, a wife is an object. Her husband can divorce her at any time without any explanation. He just has to say once or twice, "I divorce you," and that will end the marriage. If he changes his mind later, he can remarry her. If it happens in the heat of an argument, he only has to repeat three times, "I divorce you." This will end the marriage permanently, and he is not allowed to marry her again. However, there is a solution for this too. He can have his ex-wife back if he follows another set of rules with a lot of complicated procedures. First, the wife has to marry another man, and then the other man has to divorce her so she is available for the first husband to remarry. To get to this point, he has to search and find a reliable, suitable man—usually an older, handicapped, or blind man—to marry her and thereafter divorce her. For this, there are professionals called *mohallel* with track records of honesty and reliability in keeping their promises not to have sex with the divorced wives and to release them to be available to their original husbands. In turn, the mohallel will receive an amount that they have agreed to. Sometimes a mohallel falls in love with his bride, refuses to release her to the first husband, and keeps her as his legal wife, or he blackmails her husband for more money. The word mohallel means "problem solver."

The Killing of Omar

Omar's caliphate lasted ten years. He was killed by a young Persian man named Piroozan. Omar had nicknamed him "Abu-lolo," referring to his green eyes, the color of turquoise. He was separated from his family by the Arab invaders as a young boy and delivered to Medina as another present from Persia to Omar. After many years of suffering, Piroozan finally ended the life of the man who had brought chaos and misery into his life and the lives of his fellow citizens. He killed the man who had no respect for other human beings. Not only did Omar steal their goods and livelihood, he broke their spirit, pride, and dignity too. The humiliation brought by his hand left a permanent mark on the land.

Piroozan left Omar's corpse behind at his residence and got out of Medina in ample time. In Persia, he was welcomed as a great hero. As Ayesha was tirelessly on his tail, he was required to live the rest of his life in hiding. Years later, a monument was built on his gravesite. It is marked "Unknown Soldier." This is visited by a large number of patriots. It became a traditional shrine and the only symbol of resistance against the Arab invasion. Among Iranians, it is known as the Shrine of Abu-lolo and is a popular tourist attraction.

Recently the Sunni Muslims in the Arab world, who follow the caliph as the rightful leader, have put a lot of pressure on the Islamic Republic of Iran (predominantly Shiite Muslims) to demolish and dishonor this heritage building, in a way similar to what King ibn Saud of Saudi Arabia did in 1925, where he demolished the resting place and shrine of imams in Medina known as Jannat Al Baqi. This would not be acceptable to the Iranian people. The opposition to this idea is very strong. If it happened, it would be considered as another attack from Arabs on Iranian soil.

Omar's death gave a ray of hope to hopeless Persians. The day is marked in the Persian calendar as a traditional day of celebration called Omar Koshi. For the last fourteen centuries, Persians have continuously celebrated this day. It starts with a crowd of all ages meeting in an open space outside the city. The crowd follows the organizers and forms a large human circle. A live band entertains the crowd. Then a man dressed in black with a black turban, the end of which covers his face, carrying a sword, pushes the crowd aside and enters the circle. While he runs around from time to time, he charges at the crowd, which boos him. The ringmaster calls this presence "Omar." Again, the crowd reacts with hostility toward him. Then a young, tall, handsome man dressed in white jumps into the circle. The crowd gets excited, stands up, and welcomes him loudly when the ringmaster introduces him as a Persian hero. Then the two men walk fast around the ring, angrily exchanging words and slogans. Finally, they get closer and jump on each other. Every now and then, they disappear in the dust they have created. Back and forth, they continue for a while. As is expected, the young man manages to get Omar down and sit on his chest while raising his knife. He looks at the crowd as they shout, "Kill him." They jubilantly clap their hands and call death to Omar. The celebration ends with the burning of Omar's effigy.

Persia suffered major setbacks in every aspect of life under the rule of caliphs that ended in 1258. Fourteen centuries have passed since the Arab invasion. The Shiite Muslims, a branch of Islam, are searching for direction as they continuously grieve for their last imam named Mahdi, who died many centuries ago. He ran for his life and disappeared into the crowd. His followers are waiting for him to come back and guide them in the pursuit of happiness and a better life.

Osman Caliphate

The sudden death of Omar created a vacuum and instilled panic into the Arab world. His death caught Ayesha by surprise. She was not ready for his death, and she had no suitable, reliable, and aggressive person in the circle of her tribe to replace him. In a hurry, she appointed the seventy-one-year-old Othman (Osman) as the third caliph. He was a rich man and had married two of Mohammad's daughters. This earned him the special title "owner of two lights."

Osman had a rough start; it was difficult to fill the vacuum that had been created by Omar's death. Persian resistance fighters intensified their counterattacks. They saw the opportunity to reorganize and fight to free their hijacked country. Newly rich Arabs panicked that Persians would take advantage of the situation, regain their country, and exact revenge. To stop that, they did not hesitate to burn and destroy every standing city and village and wipe them off the map. Hassan and Hussein, Ali's sons and Mohammad's grandchildren from his daughter Fatima, played a leading role in that massacre, so cruel that rivers of blood ran everywhere through the ruins.

While all this was happening, Ayesha had another important duty to fulfill. For a long time, it had been one of her priorities to create a religious book for the promotion and spread of the new religion. For every religion, a holy book is a message from God, and the new religion of Islam didn't yet have one. Twenty-four years after the death of Mohammad, she gave Osman the assignment to create a holy book while he was busy doing other things, including fighting Persian resistance fighters. Finally, after twelve years, he had the book ready. At the time of its presentation to Ayesha, he claimed that he did not believe in the authenticity of book or that these were the words of Allah sent through his messenger.

This made him a target and cast a shadow of death over him. Ayesha, with the help of her brother Abdullah, brutally killed the eighty-three-year-old man at his residence and left his corpse to rot for days. In the end, she did not allow Osman's body to be buried in a Muslim graveyard. Instead, he was buried in a Jewish cemetery. Years later, after Ayesha's death, his remains were moved to Jannat Al Baqi, a burial site in Saudi Arabia.

Ali as Imam

Ayesha had to look for the next candidate to lead the territories that were ruled by caliphs. Persia was now a bankrupt country with hopeless, poor people who had terrible experiences with caliphs. Before Ayesha chose another person to continue the same acts of discrimination against them, they suggested Ali. Firstly, he was the cousin and son-in-law of Mohammad, and secondly, they wanted Ali and his sons Hassan and Hussein, the leading and effective fighters against Persian resistance fighters, to be on their side to stop the fighting and bring peace and unity.

Choosing Ali did not sit well with Ayesha. To her, Ali was a good fighter, but he was not qualified to be a caliph. He was an uneducated man who had spent most of his life as a shepherd, driving herds, day in, day out, to the pasture. Besides, she thought it was her right to choose the caliph and not the right of the losers and the people she had no respect for. She did not accept Ali as caliph. Therefore, Persians renamed him "Imam," a leader with limited power. He was the spiritual leader of their new faith, Shiism. All the future imams have been descendants of Mohammad; most of them were born, lived, and died in Saudi Arabia. The last imam disappeared in 874.

Sunni Islam continues to follow caliphs as their political, military, and spiritual leaders. Their headquarters was first based in Medina, then moved to Syria, and later moved to Baghdad, Iraq, the center of their activity.

Ali became a mouthpiece of the Persians. This made Ayesha nervous and angry—nervous because Persia might escape from under her thumb and angry that they used Ali as a shield to protect them from her force. She thought this could be the first step in Persia becoming independent. It was clear to the Persians that Ayesha would not hesitate to get rid of Ali and choose another caliph, which would be another disaster for Persia. Ali respected Ayesha but could not trust her or ignore her ruthlessness. He reached out to her and asked for peace and friendship, but Ayesha wanted him out of her way, so she prepared a battle against him.

Finally, in the year 656, she and her army arrived in Basra, Iraq, to fight and capture Ali. To her surprise, Ali was awaiting her arrival with an army that included Persian resistance fighters. This became a famous battle, called the Battle of the Camel, because she was riding on a camel to view the battle in which she eventually was badly defeated. This incident made her panic again, and she was more anxious than ever to finish the job of getting rid of Ali. She planned and set the stage for his execution and then sent a message to him: "Now I am ready for peace and invite you to come for a peace talk." Against the advice of the Persians, Ali made the trip there. He was offered a seat with his back to a curtain. A killer with a poisoned saber attacked him from behind and split his skull in two. He was buried in Najaf, Iraq.

The outrage and anger over Ali's death set off a string of protests from the opposition. It was the only time Persians could gather to mourn openly without resistance. This continued for days and weeks. Mourners turned the death of Ali into an unusual show of anger against Ayesha and her unpopular caliph. Over time, the continuation of this behavior changed the culture of festivity and life enjoyment that Persians knew into a mood of permanent mourning, sorrow, and grief. For Ayesha, the five years of Ali's imamate were a waste of time in the advancement of her husband's dream. By now, she was an embattled forty-five-year-old woman looking for somebody capable to continue to hold the territories captured by Omar under her watch.

Muawiyya's Caliphate

Ayesha's last resort was to turn to Muawiyya for help. He was from the Umayyad dynasty ruling in Damascus, Syria. Umayyad was from the same tribe as Mohammad but from a different clan. Ayesha delivered all the spoils that Omar had vacuumed from Persia into Medina, now delivered to Damascus, Syria. With it, she passed the leash of Persia into the hands of Syria. In return, she asked Umayyad dynasty to be renamed a caliphate and Muawiyya to become the fourth caliph. Delivering the Persian loot from Medina to Damascus by Ayesha would cut the imams' power and make the imams poor and helpless. Over time, many of the Shiite imams in Medina had been poisoned on the orders of their rival caliphs ruling in Baghdad, Iraq.

Umayyad continued to rule in an atmosphere of mistrust, fear, and hopelessness. This is a sample of a letter Muawiyya wrote to his half-brother, who was the governor of the provinces of Pars and Khuzestan in southwest Persia:

> If you want to make your job easier, do what Omar did to this folk, who were called "Ajams" [Persians]. Keep them under constant pressure. They are always wrong even if they are right. Take their advice but don't give them credit. Keep your distance and never listen to their complaints. Never laugh or enjoy time in their presence. Always give them half of what they are supposed to get. In prayer, they should stay behind Arabs and never be allowed in the front row.

The above guidance has been passed from one caliph ruler to the next throughout the Umayyad dynasty, and it later also continued through the Abbasid caliphate. Under such an atmosphere and mentality, young males born by Persian women, who had been brought from Persia to Arabian countries and sold as sex slaves, started to migrate to their motherland. Persia did not welcome them and resisted their presence because, firstly, their pure Persian blood had been contaminated with Arab. Secondly, they were born out of wedlock, which is a shameful thing and against Persian tradition. Instead, this became a golden opportunity for the Arabs to welcome them and create effective allies against the Persians. Therefore, they raised the status of these young men and made them superior to the rest of the Persian population.

To isolate them from the rest and not implement the Muawiyya's guidelines, they were given the title of *sayyed* that raised their status to children of the prophet. This title was given to them by the Arabs. With time, this became part of the Shiite belief. Sayyeds are visually recognized by the fact that they wear a green turban or a green shawl wrapped around their bellies.

They came to their motherland because:

- All the girls born to captured Persian women had been buried alive after birth.
- Persia was rebuilding itself, which gave them job opportunities.
- They were bilingual. This would help them to get government and administrative jobs.

The title of sayyed would give them an advantage over the rest. This title is hereditary; it passes from one generation to the next. Because of its great benefits, many false claims to these titles were made. As the time passed, their numbers have grown substantially. The phenomenon of sayyed is part of Shiite Islam only, and Iran's spiritual leader, Ali Khamenei, carries this title. It would be an insult not to call him "Sayyed Ali Khamenei." In any Shiite Islamic society, a sayyed ranks at the top and an infidel at the bottom. Poor or rich, good or bad, other Muslims rank in between. An infidel can never prevail against a sayyed.

Once, a lone stranger had occupied a Zartoshti's farm and made the farmer's storage shed his home. The farmer had no power to get rid of him and take back the control of his own property. He hired a few Muslims to remove the trespasser. When the first negotiations didn't work, they forcefully pushed the door open. To their surprise, the first thing they saw was a green shawl wrapped around the stranger's big belly. This came as a shock to everybody. Their immediate reaction was, "Oh my god, a sayyed. The Prophet Child is living in such a miserable place." Until then nobody knew his name, which was Sayyed Khalegh. It was not good news for the farm owner. He noticed that his presence was not wanted; he turned back and left the place quietly. As the word spread, everybody wanted to have a chance to help make up to the lonely, poor sayyed. It was a blessing and a pass for going to heaven. They delivered food and clothing to him, even though many didn't have enough for themselves and their children. From then on, he was living a heaven on earth.

One of the women, out of love for Allah, became pregnant by him. She surprised her husband with the news that they were having another child. He became suspicious and very angry, and he threatened her with death. To save her life, she told the truth—that she was pregnant by Sayyed Khalegh. Traditionally, in a case like this, honor killing would be the only option. It has happened that a Muslim only imagined that his wife was sleeping with another man and for that reason would beat, punish, and even kill her. But here, an unborn sayyed was involved. This complicated the matter. It was unthinkable that a Muslim husband would live with his wife when she was pregnant by somebody else. On the other hand, he would definitely go to hell if he harmed the unborn baby sayyed. Not only that, it was a blessing to have a sayyed being born in his household.

The case of Sayyed Khalegh was passed to the village elders; it became an argument between the husband and sayyed. The wife was not included in the testimony, because her words did not carry any weight. She was hiding with her relatives and waiting for the outcome. The final verdict, as was expected, was that the husband should divorce his pregnant wife and that she should marry Sayyed Khalegh.

It was time for the sayyed to show his birth certificate and true identity. The way he was acting, and the fact that he disagreed with the verdict and claimed the child was not his, raised suspicion. Under heavy pressure from the court of elders, he took off and disappeared as mysteriously as he had come to this place in the middle of desert. Later, authorities found out he was a fugitive with no connection to sayyed-hood.

The result was an immediate death sentence for the pregnant woman. To end this dilemma, an old man volunteered to marry her and raise the child with the money collected by the woman's relatives, arranging their escape to the big city of Tehran where nobody could find them. There she attempted to have an abortion, helped by a housewife who was recommended by her new neighbor. Because she was five-and-a-half months pregnant, she was told that the fetus first had to be destroyed, and then removed from her womb. This was done with a bicycle spoke, which caused her great agony, and she died from the infection.

Continuation of Imams

Persia continued to be ruled by caliphs as political leaders and their own imams as spiritual leaders. An imam is born to his profession, and after his death, his resting place becomes a Shiite shrine (*imam zadahe*). When Ali passed away, his older son Hassan became the second imam. He tried to play a balancing act between Persia and the Umayyad rulers in Syria. At this time, Muawiyya died, and his son Yazid was named the fifth caliph. Hassan, the new imam, became Ayesha's target too and her next victim. To get rid of him, Ayesha promised Hassan's wife Asama, "If you poison your husband, I will arrange your marriage to Caliph Yazid." Hassan died quietly at the age of forty-seven. This time, there was no opportunity for the Persians to mourn his death. Ayesha's hate for imams prevented Hassan from being buried next to his grandfather Mohammad. Instead, he was buried at Jannat Al Baqi in Medina.

Ayesha continued to work as an important advisor to the caliphs in Syria. As much as she supported the caliphs, she was against the imams. Her work continued until she died at the age of sixty-five. Her death and her final resting place have been kept secret. In Persia, to insult a woman, call her "Ayesha."

As mentioned before, Islam started with Mohammad's first wife, Khadijah, and his third wife, Ayesha, kept it going. This proves that women in the pre-Islamic era had more freedom, rights, and equality than afterward. Persian women had been equal to men in all aspects of life, from decision-making to administrative and higher jobs. As they converted to Islam, Muslim women lost their rights. They were downgraded to sex symbols and became victims of the impractical sharia law.

The next person in line for the imamate was Hussein, the younger son of Ali. He became the third imam. Hussein didn't want to live in the shadow of Caliph Yazid. He was the grandson of Mohammad and had been at the forefront in every fight against Persia. He chose to stand up to Caliph Yazid and fight for his rightful position as a caliph. He wanted to revoke what Ayesha had done and return wealth and power from Syria back to its original rightful owner—Mohammad's family in Medina. Therefore, he got involved in an uphill battle against the rich and powerful Yazid. He felt confident in starting this fight because he was counting heavily on Persian support, but that didn't materialize.

When Hussein arrived in Basra, Iraq, with a small group of men and his family, he asked for the commitment of the Persians to help him defeat Yazid, just like they helped his father Ali to defeat Ayesha in the Battle of the Camel. This time the Persians had no interest or reason to get involved in a conflict between two Arab groups fighting for power: Hussein, their imam who had a lot of Persian blood on his hands, and

Yazid, a caliph supported by Ayesha. There had been no love lost from either side toward Persia. Finally, in Karbala, Hussein and his men came face to face with Yazid's army. There was no actual combat; the only action that was taken was to make sure Hussein and his fighters had no access to water. In the end, they died from dehydration.

As was expected, when the news of Hussein's death reached Persia, he was elevated to martyr, which was followed by a grand demonstration and long-lasting mourning. It was more a statement to show their anger and hate against Ayesha's actions than sincere grief for Hussein's death. Hussein was buried in Karbala, Iraq, where he died. His grave became an important Shiite shrine. Every year on the ninth day of the month of Moharam, thousands of Shiites visit the site. Saddam Hussein, a Sunni leader, opposed the Shiite pilgrimages. He closed the gate and stopped the pilgrims from visiting the site. From childhood, Saddam was taught by his uncle to hate the Persians, whom he called *Ajam* (a nickname by Arabs for Persia). He always quoted his uncle, who said, "Three things God should have not created: the Jew, the fly, and the Ajam." To stop the large numbers of Ajam flocking into his land every year, he demolished Imam Hussein's shrine and turned it into flat farmland. After Saddam Hussein's death, the Iranian Islamic regime spent a large amount of oil revenue to build an expensive mosque with a real gold dome on the original site. After Hussein, his son Ali Zainul Abedin, King Yazdegerd's grandson from his captured daughter Shahrbanu, born in Medina, became the fourth imam. He had been sick and was mentally unstable. It has been said that he acted that way to be immune from the caliph's sword. In the end, he was poisoned by Caliph Waleed in AD 729 at the age of fifty-eight and buried in Medina in Jannat Al Baqi.

The fifth imam, Mohammad Baqir, was born in Medina. He was poisoned by Caliph al-Malik and buried in Jannat Al Baqi. Both Shiite and Sunni Muslims accepted him as an expert in Islamic law (sharia). His popularity and influence had grown to the point where it became intolerable to Caliph al-Malik. Mohammad Baqir died painfully three days after his saddle was covered with poison. His son Jafar Sadegh, the sixth imam, lived in a violent time. Many of his relatives had been massacred at the hands of the Umayyad caliphs because they were considered rebels. He himself was later poisoned by Caliph al-Mansur. He was born in Medina and died at the age of thirty-seven. He was also buried in Jannat Al Baqi in Medina.

Traditionally, after Jafar Sadegh, his older son Ishmael should have positioned himself as the seventh imam of Shi'i. This didn't happen because the people around him thought he was not mentally suited for this task and that he was not in a position to answer questions and guide

67

his followers. Many Shiites chose his younger brother Moussa instead. Others followed the tradition and stayed with the elder son, Ishmael. This caused Shiite Islam to branch into two. Ishmael's followers are known as Ismaili. They became a minority and subject to discrimination and constant pressure from Moussa's followers. They left Persia for Afghanistan and India. Since 1818, under the leadership of Aga Khan, they've built a successful community. From India, they moved to African countries, particularly Uganda. When President Idi Amin started harassing all foreigners in his country, including Ismailis, they had to leave their good lives in Africa and immigrate to Canada and the United States. There they built their own mosques and lived peacefully with the rest of the citizens. They started their own businesses, sometimes with the support of the Aga Khan Foundation.

The branch under Moussa continued and ended at the twelfth imam. Therefore, they are called Shiite Twelve Imamis. Moussa had thirty-seven children: nineteen daughters and eighteen sons. He was imprisoned by Caliph Harun al-Rashid. Four years later, the caliph ordered him to be poisoned. His body is resting in Iraq. His thirty-five-year-old son, Al Raida (Reza), became the eighth Imam. He was born in 765 in Medina and was poisoned by Caliph Mammon. He died at the age of sixty-two. He is the only imam who was buried in Persia. His grave is inside the tomb of Caliph Harun al-Rashid near the city of Mashad. This place is one of the Shiite's most popular and profitable shrines. Pilgrims from all corners of the country visit the place. They come here to ask Imam Reza to cure their illnesses and make their wishes come true. To make sure it will happen, they must donate money to him. The money ends up in the government's coffers.

Al Askari was the eleventh spiritual leader of Persian Shiite Islam. He was born in Medina but lived close to his subjects in Iraq. None of the imams had been allowed to live in Persia, because Iraq was the center of power when caliphs ruled over Persia, Iraq, and Syria. In the six years of his imamate, he was mostly restricted and under house arrest. He died from poisoning on the order of Caliph Al Mutated. After his death, his nine-year-old son Mohammad al-Askari was made the twelfth imam. At the age of ten, he was called to Baghdad by the caliph. There, he received information that the worst was awaiting him. To save his life, he escaped and disappeared into the crowd. However, the caliph had secretly planned to ambush and kill the boy without taking the blame and angering his followers. The Shiite believed that he was hiding in a well and waiting for the right moment to show up. Days, months, and years passed. His followers waited for the young imam to be found and returned home. At some point, they accepted that he was missing, but not dead. Therefore, they called him Imam-e-ghaem (hidden imam).

Years later, they accepted his permanent absence and, eventually, his death. At this point, the Persians acknowledged that it didn't make sense for the Shiite to choose another imam. The last imam was renamed from Ghaem to Imam-e-Zaman (permanent imam). Later, this was changed again to Imam-e-Mahdi (the guided imam) who will return before the Day of Judgment and guide the forces of good against evil. He will lead his followers in pursuit of happiness and a beautiful life. Iran's President Ahmadinejad is a devout follower of this belief. Once in parliament, he defended his deputy who was accused of being an infidel. In the deputy's defense, Ahmadinejad explained that at dinner, his deputy set an extra dish of food on the table for Imam Mahdi, in case he showed up.

Umayyad Expansion

Muawiyya, the founder of the Umayyad dynasty in 661, was ruling from Syria over the Arabic-speaking Middle East, including Persia. They had no ambitions or hope to promote Islam in Persia. Instead, they turned their attention to predominantly Arabic-speaking countries like Egypt, which has its roots in civilization, and has suffered the same way as Persia from the hand of Omar, who acted like the modern Taliban by destroying all signs and traces of past civilization, specifically burning books and libraries. Umayyad started to promote Islam in poor African countries along the Mediterranean coast, riding on Persian wealth and a religious book written in Arabic—their native language. Muawiyya progressed along the African coast all the way to Morocco and Tunisia.

It was an easy, successful mission. This encouraged them to advance further. In AD 719, Arabs continued through the Strait of Gibraltar into Spain. The new religion, which they initially thought was meant only for Arabs, now had the opportunity to expand further. With great caution, they moved gradually forward. Unlike during the invasion of Persia, they started with positive and caring attitudes, with a great deal of contribution to the host country. As they moved forward, they built roads, bridges, schools, and mosques, created jobs, and raised people's standards of living. Systematically, with ease, they passed through Spain and into part of France. When they arrived in Sicily in the south of Italy, the alarm went off. The Roman leader noticed and remembered the tragedy that his counterpart, the king of Persia, had gone through. Rome acted swiftly, and with the help of other European nations, pushed the Arabs back to their original port of entry in Gibraltar; from there, they crossed the Strait of Gibraltar to arrive back in Africa.

The last Umayyad caliph, Marwan II, reigned from 744–750. He was a weak ruler, with low popularity, and opposition to him grew stronger. The anti-Umayyad contingent and their leader, Abbas, gained strength. Abbas was a descendant of Prophet Mohammad and more in line with imams. This move took power from the Umayyad caliphate back into the hands of the imam's family. Abbasid caliphs ruled from Baghdad in Iraq over Syria and Persia for the next five hundred and thirty-five years.

About the ninth century, during the Abbasid caliphate, the first Persian dynasty since the conquest by the Arabs was created in Khorasan, a province in the northeast of Persia, and named Samanid. This name came from its founder, Saman-Khoda, who was a Tajik from the city of Balkh (the birthplace of Zoroastrian prophet Zartosht). Within a short period of time, Khorasan enjoyed prosperity and expanded industry and cultural life under the Samanid dynasty. Writers and political thinkers reappeared. Khorasan became the center of great patronage of the Persian language and art. The writers made all the effort to purge Arabic words from the Persian language and use only the native language of Farsi. Roodaki and Ferdosi were the greatest poets of their time. *Shahnameh*, the world's longest epic poetry, was written by Ferdosi with only Persian words. He had patronized the Persian culture and language.

In AD 1060, the Seljuk Turks originated from Turkey and defeated the Samanids, and over the years they expanded their territory from Turkey, over Khorasan, and up to Sind and Punjab in India. In 1219, the invasion and onslaught by force of Mongols led by Genghis Khan devastated Persia again. The only positive outcome was that the Mongols put an end to the Seljuks, who had occupied part of Persia, and at the same time freed Persia after centuries from an Islamic state and caliphate. One-third of Persia's population vanished, because the main source of water and the irrigation systems were destroyed. This caused famine and natural disease. A plague known as the Black Death wiped out three-quarters, or fifteen million, of the country's population.

Mongols started to rule with Mongolian rules and laws. Later, they made the city of Samarkand, which was an important center of art, their capital city, and gradually adopted Persian traditions and laws. One of their leaders fell in love with the Persian culture and tradition. He asked for conversion from Buddhism to Islam. What he received was the Sunni version, which he later carried to Indonesia, Malaysia, and other Asian countries. In 1255, Mongol forces invaded Syria and Palestine. In 1258, they captured Baghdad, destroyed the city, and ended centuries of caliphate rule.

Timur, a descendant of Genghis Khan, had expanded his territory to an area the size of today's Middle East. He ruled from 1370–1405.

His dynasty lasted until 1500. Timur appointed his sons and grandsons to govern the different parts of the empire. The cost of Timur's conquests amounted to seven million deaths. By 1500, Timur's empire had lost control of most territories, and Persia fell to the Safavid dynasty.

Persian Dynasties

The Safavid dynasty included the first Persian rulers after the Arab conquest of Persia. They ruled over all of Persia and most of the Middle East. In 1501, Ismail appeared among the Turkish-speaking people from Ardabil and, with the help of the Turkmen tribe, captured Tabriz from the neighboring Uzbek confederation west of the Caspian Sea, and he became the founder of the Safavid dynasty. At the age of thirteen, he was enthroned as shah of Azerbaijan (a province in the northeast of Persia). In May of the following year, he also became shah of Persia. He claimed to be a descendant of the Prophet Mohammad on his father's side, and also he had the last royal Sassanid blood—both via Hussein, the grandson of Mohammad, who married Shahrbanu, the daughter of the last Persian king, Yazdegerd.

He adopted the Shi'a brand of Islam as the country's official religion, regained most parts of Iraq, including the cities of Baghdad and Mosul, and added the most important holy cities of Najaf and Karbala in Iraq to Persia. His Sunni rival, the Turkish Ottoman sultan, Selim, congratulated him on this victory and advised him not to destroy the graves and mosques of the Sunni Muslims there. Ismail ignored this advice and intensified his opposition to Sunni Muslims. It was Shah Ismail who ordered "the ritual cursing of the first three caliphs (Abu Bakr, Omar, and Osman) at the end of each Friday praying time." The tension between him and Sultan Selim grew. In 1514, he was defeated by Sultan Selim and then moved his capital city from Tabriz further south to Qazvin. He died in 1526 at the age of thirty-eight.

Safavid kings left legacies behind by constructing monuments, buildings, and mosques. Shah Abbas Square in Isfahan is one of Shah Abbas's legacies and a famous tourist attraction. To please Britain, Shah Abbas allowed Christians to practice their religion freely. This helped Armenians to escape execution by the Turks and settle in Isfahan and the northwest of Persia.

Shah Sultan Hussein, the last Safavid king, who ruled from 1694 to 1722, has been described as the most incompetent king of the Safavid dynasty. When he became shah, he immediately appointed a head mullah called Majlesi to the newly established office of *mullah bashi* and made him responsible for the daily affairs of running the country. The shah himself retreated to his harem with his wives. Under the guidance of Majlesi, Shiite rituals, such as the mourning for Imam Hussein, reached their highpoint, and this continues to the present time.

Majlesi's policies also included the persecution of Zoroastrians and other infidels. He forced them to convert to Shi'a Islam or they would be executed. The city of Isfahan, with a population of over seventy thousand Zartoshti, went into a panic. To survive, a large number changed from Zartoshti to Shi'a Islam. Some resisted Islam and were therefore massacred. The rest disappeared into the desert around Yazd and Kerman. The latter group continues to live here in a very harsh climate, where water and fertile land is scarce. It took a lot of effort to be able to survive in such an environment. They created miles of irrigation system of canals to bring water from the foot of the mountains to the farmland. Even there, they continued to be harassed and threatened by homegrown fanatic Muslims. A Zartoshti farmer would have difficulty in delivering his goods to market. Usually he would be harassed by the merchant and shopkeeper for walking barefoot on the wet surface. In their presence, a farmer was not allowed to ride on his farm animal. Anything wet a *kafar* (non-Muslim) touches should be avoided by a Muslim. It would be suicidal for a non-Muslim to enter any public water storage. The Jews have been treated the same way as the

Zoroastrians. Out of necessity a bond was formed between the two to work together to fill the gap for the services that were not allowed by Muslims to them.

Shaban, a middle-aged Jew carrying a backpack, walks miles from the Jewish quarter in the southeast of the city of Yazd to each village in a radius of two to six miles. On his arrival, he knocks on the door of Zartoshtis that he passes by and calls, "Shaban is here!" If there is no answer, he continues to the next house. In some villages, Zartoshti and Muslims live side by side. The Zartoshtis who have converted to Islam continue to live in their family homes. Shaban is a barber; he cuts hair and does the shaving. In his backpack, he carries a hammer and pliers to repair shoes; with the same plier, he also pulls teeth. Usually Zoroastrians don't practice circumcision, but if there is a demand, Shaban will do it with his sharp shaving knife. Often when on his way, he is harassed and beaten by

Muslims for making and selling alcoholic beverages. He makes these in his backyard. He dumps leftover fruits, vegetables, and other plant material into a pond and then leaves it for few months to ferment. The mix will be distilled with a kettle and a homemade pipe to produce the final product called "Shaban," which is similar to vodka. Because of the nature of his job, he is in contact with Zoroastrians in every village. In his mind, he has a network of young people whom he has known from childhood and who now are at the age to form families. This has made him a matchmaker. He walks fast. He is a good listener and not much of a talker.

The pressure and discrimination from homegrown Muslims drove the Zoroastrians to seek adventure and discover alternative places to live. A few brave men left their families behind and went east toward India. They put their faith and lives in the hands of some tough and dangerous Baluchis to guide them through the Afghan Mountains and passes to arrive illegally in India. Baluchis live in Baluchistan in the southeast of Persia. Because of its harsh climate, their men were famous for being tough and good fighters. It was their principle that if one of their companions got sick or wounded—for instance, from falling off a mountain—the rest should continue, leaving him behind, and never look back.

After part of India divided into Pakistan, a Muslim domain, Zoroastrian immigrants moved further east to India, with their final destination the city of Bombay. For the Zoroastrians, this was the land of freedom and opportunity. It was common practice to start as a busboy in a tea shop or restaurant, working long hours and sleeping on the sidewalks to save money. Often, when the men were asleep, rats would chew the hard skin off the heels of their feet. Their ultimate goal was to own their own businesses. This would give them the status and freedom to go back to visit their wives and children and return legally to India by ship. Through hard work and honesty, they built a good reputation in their host country. The Indian government recognized and appreciated their presence as great assets. This paved the road for others to follow and be welcomed to the new homeland. In India, they are known as Parsis. At the beginning of the twentieth century, Reza Shah, the founder of the Pahlavi dynasty, gave freedom of religion to minorities, and made it possible for Parsis to come back to their homeland. Some of them came back with enough money to contribute to the progress and building of a new Iran. Education was their priority; therefore, they built schools in the villages for girls and boys.

Education was available to all, but only a small percentage of Muslim boys took advantage of the pathway out of illiteracy. In India, the word *Parsi* became a symbol of respect and wealth. Within a short time span, Parsis in India created jobs and built factories, schools, and hospitals. Many of them became rich and famous. Now, two-thirds of the world's Zoroastrians live in India. They practice their own religion and live in peace and harmony, side by side with the other Indian citizens. Most of them didn't want go back to Iran, because after generations, their language changed from Parsi to Urdu. In their absence, Shah Sultan Hussein confiscated their land and assets and used this as state treasure to build mosques and pay for British officers.

In 1722, the Safavid dynasty was defeated and their reign was put to an end by invasions from neighboring Afghanistan. Five years later, Nadir, a Safavid general, rose to power. He defeated the Afghans and at the same time expelled the Ottomans and Russians who were occupying the northern part of the country. Nadir became king and founder of the Afshar dynasty. He captured Delhi in 1738 and was killed by his entourage on his way back from victory. Then, for forty years, Persia was ruled by the Zandiah dynasty, founded by Karim Khan Zand. He was one of Nadir Shah's generals. He followed the policy of the Safavid dynasty; he also was instrumental in increasing the British influence in the country and improved the judicial system to the civilized Western system.

After the death of Karim Khan Zand, the country plunged into disorder. Agha Mohammad Khan Qajar, of Mongol descent, in 1795 proclaimed himself the king of Persia from the Qajar dynasty and made the city of Tehran, with a population of twenty thousand, his capital.

Agha Mohammad Khan Qajar was castrated at the age of six. Despite being a eunuch, he was a tribal chief. He was known to be a most cruel ruler. He is famous for the fact that after the long siege of the city of Kerman, he ordered his soldiers to punish the residents by taking out the eyes of twenty thousand men and killing four thousand others, before setting the city on fire. He was afraid that he would be assassinated by his family; therefore, he put some of them to death and made others blind.

This did not stop him from being assassinated within three years of coming in power. He was assassinated one night in 1797 when he was visiting the city of Shusha. A quarrel arose between a servant and the valet; they raised their voices high. The shah became angry and upset; he ordered them to be executed. Since it was a Friday (the Islamic holy day), the shah postponed their executions to the next day and ordered them to go back to their duties. They knew what was going to happen to them, and in their desperation, they invaded the royal pavilion while the shah was sleeping and murdered him with a dagger and knife. He was succeeded by his nephew Fath Ali Shah Qajar, who declared a holy war against Russia and lost Armenia and Azerbaijan.

Nasser-e-Din Shah, another Qajar king, reigned over Persia for forty-eight years (1848–1896). He was the first Persian king to travel to

Europe and make reforms by curbing the secular power of the clergy. He made a treaty with his rival, the Sunni Muslim Ottoman Empire, to stop the further expansion of Russia in the north. In turn, at the request of the Ottomans, he stopped the ritual cursing and condemnation of Caliph Omar.

During the Qajar dynasty, in 1844, a merchant named Sayyed Mohammad Shirazi, known as Báb, claimed to be God's messenger. His follower Bábis believed he was the Mahdi, of whom the Shiite Muslim were eagerly awaiting the reappearance. Initially, some Shi'i Muslims accepted this new religion. Along with them came some Jews and Zartoshti who had been resisting Islam. They saw the opportunity to jump on the bandwagon as a path to freedom and relief from Farrash Bashi, who had the power to demand any amount of *jayziah* (an infidel tax).

Bábis had a rough time from the beginning. A clash between them and the authorities ended with the order of the then-king Nasser-e-Din Shah to follow these faithful and execute them. Two years later, a plan by radical Bábis in retaliation to assassinate the shah failed. This was followed by the onslaught of thousands of Bábis to the point of their extinction. One of Báb's followers named Mirza Hussein Nuri claimed he was the new prophet who had been foretold by Báb. Most of Báb's followers joined him and continued the teaching of Báb. Mirza Hussein was renamed Bahá Allah and his followers were called Bahá'ís. Their teaching is written in a mix of Arabic and Farsi. Nasser-e-Din Shah was assassinated by a follower of Al-Afghan while praying in the famous shrine of Shah Abdol Azim. He is buried in the same shrine.

Bahá'ís are very active and easily give up their lives to promote this new religion. The main point of their argument is that religion is similar to school; every prophet in his own time preaches like a teacher to prepare students for the next grade and for a new teacher. Their prophets are the most recent teachers, and therefore, the world should accept and learn their teachings, because their laws and messages are for modern civilization. They believe in all other of God's messengers, including the ones before theirs, such as Mohammad. Bahá'ís reject jihad and promote peace and harmony among all nations, and their slogan reads, "One world, one god, and one religion."

Unfortunately, with the current regime in Iran, it turned out that the newly converted Bahá'í have jumped from the frying pan into the fire. After the Islamic revolution in 1979, pressure grew on minority religions, especially Bahá'ís, who were blacklisted and subjected to persecution. According to the Islamic Republic's supreme leader, Sayyed Ali Khamenei, "They must be rooted out all over the world." Under his regime, nobody should hire Bahá'í, and their children are banned from attending any school. Bahá'ís are harmless fanatics who easily give up their lives and walk like lambs to the slaughterhouse for the cause of promoting their religion. The gap between death and life is just one word, yes or no. Usually, when interrogated, a Bahá'í will be asked, "Are you Bahá'í?" and almost always the answer is yes. He or she is then killed and joins the *yaran* (martyrs), and he or she will always be remembered with his or her name and a picture with every Bahá'í family. If he or she chooses to say no, the Bahá'í will escape the persecution, but the consequence is that he or she will be shunned and excluded from friends, family, and others within the Bahá'í community.

Pahlavi Dynasty

In 1921, Reza Khan, an army officer, ended the Qajar dynasty with a coup d'état while the last Qajar king, the eleven-year old Mohammad Ali Shah, was on holiday in southern France. Reza Khan became Reza Shah, the founder of the Pahlavi dynasty. He started to rebuild the country, which had been neglected and had stayed backward for many centuries. His mission was to close the gap that had existed for fourteen centuries between his country and Western civilization and bring it into the twentieth century. He had the vision and plans to do it. Within the short time of twenty years of his rule, he established the authority and power to suppress the mullahs and religious leaders, who had been obstacles for many years, in order to move the country forward. He gave Persian women the same rights and freedoms they had had in the pre-Islamic era. He eliminated the chador (hijab) and forbade women to wear it.

With the help of Germany and German engineers, he continued industrializing the country on a grand scale, implementing major infrastructure projects: construction of a cross-country railroad system, providing national public education, sending young Persians to Europe for higher education, reforming the judiciary system from Islamic sharia law to modern civil law, and improving health care by building hospitals with modern equipment, mostly run by doctors who had returned after their education in foreign countries. He realized most of his dream within the first sixteen years of his ruling.

In 1935, he changed the name of Persia to Iran (Aryan), which was the name of the original race that occupied Persia. This move almost disconnected thousands of years of culture and civilization that has been associated with the name of Persia.

During the Second World War, Reza Shah tried to stay neutral. He had signed a thirty-year contract with the British to make sure the oil money would continue to support his projects. The British presence through ownership of the British-Persia (BP) Oil Company prevented Reza Shah from continuing to obtain technical assistance from other European countries. They claimed that the Germans in Iran were spies with a mission to sabotage the oil facilities. The shah, under pressure from the British, expelled all Germans from Iran. This almost stopped the progress of industrialization and project development. Finally, in August 1941, Great Britain and the Soviet Union invaded and occupied Iran with a massive military assault. They arrested Reza Shah and sent him into exile in Johannesburg, South Africa, replacing him with a softer leader, his son Mohammad Reza.

The young shah's plan was to continue his father's work and policies. In 1951, the Iranian people advocated support for nationalizing the country's oil. This popular movement started with Iran's Prime Minister Dr. Mohammad Mossadegh and won the support of the majority of Iranians. The shah liked the idea but could not break the contract with Britain to support the movement. He was worried that the West would embargo Iranian oil—the only source of income for the country. It would be a great setback for Iran's economy and its development projects. His position isolated him from the majority of the country's population. Under heavy pressure from the Toodeh (Communist) party and the mullahs, he left the country.

This created a vacuum between the Persian Gulf in the south and the Soviet Union in the north. It was the height of the Cold War and Russia sought to fill the gap. Britain and the United States were afraid of communism and the expansion of the Soviet Union. They reinstated the shah and put Prime Minister Mossadegh under house arrest. All this weakened the Shah's power and authority. He was called the puppet of foreign leaders. This gave the mullahs an opportunity to come into action; they had been dormant for some time.

Revolution of 1979

The stage was set for a revolution in Iran. People started robbing banks, setting fire to movie theaters, burning buildings and businesses, closing bazaars, and kidnapping and raping women—all this to create fear and panic in the heart of common citizens. This terrorist action continued with little or no resistance. The shah's hands were tied by the human rights watchdog who acted on order of some foreign leaders. The shah was in charge of the world petroleum organization (OPEC). This made him unpopular among Western leaders who were in favor of cheap oil.

He listened to his people's voices who were calling day and night on the roofs, "Allah-o-Akbar," an Arabic phrase meaning "God is great." With his experience as a responsible leader, he was not willing to be involved in bloodshed against his own people. With sadness, he gave up his throne and left the country.

Eventually, the Islamic Republic of Iran became an alternative to the Pahlavi dynasty. This was supported by the faithful and the participation of the majority of Iranians. At the beginning, there was a lot of excitement and enthusiasm. The air was full of promises, hope, and change. People were eagerly looking forward for the arrival of the man of God, Khomeini, who was exiled to Paris at the time, waiting for peace and justice to arrive.

These are the messages sent by Khomeini from Paris to the Iranian people:

- God-given natural resources will be distributed evenly among the citizens, especially *mostazafin* (the poorest of poor), who have been suffering and neglected for a long time.

- The majority, consisting of the working and middle classes, will get their share of oil money.

- Everyone will have an easy, happy life, without hassle and worry.

- The check from the oil money will arrive at the end of each month to the mailboxes.

- Plenty of food will be on everybody's table.

- Nobody has to worry about the next day or, for that matter, the rest of his or her life.

- It will be like paradise on earth.

- All this will happen only under one condition: the shah must leave.

As for the rich, they knew what was coming; they took their money and left the country.

On his arrival, Khomeini received the title of imam while he was stepping down from the airplane in Tehran; the joy and excitement brought tears into the eyes of eagerly waiting followers. As soon as he was established, the first, most urgent job was to capture the shah and bring him back to Iran. He began to chase him and make demands that people hand the shah over to him for personal revenge. He took over the American embassy with its staff as hostages and then threatened to punish the countries that gave protection to the shah, blackmailing them with an oil cut.

Western countries one after the other, followed his order and rejected the shah's presence in their countries. This gave extra power to the Islamic regime and showed the weakness and submission of the Western superpowers. Then followed the rise of terrorists, Al Quaida, ISIS, and many other branches.

The revolution of 1979 marked the start of the so-called Islamic Republic of Iran. From the beginning, Khomeini made it clear that he did not have the interest and well-being of the Iranian people at heart. He was clearly a crusader of Shi'i Islam. He always repeated, "What the shah and his father have done to Iran has been un-Islamic." His plan was to stop and reverse the progress and go back to the laws and living of the seventh century AD. He strongly believed in this idea that he decided to export a similar revolution to other misguided countries, such as Saudi Arabia, Jordan, Egypt, Iraq, and all other countries around the Persian Gulf.

To his surprise, in his first attempt at an international revolution, he came face to face with Saddam Hussein, the Iraqi president. Their encounter triggered an eight-year war that was fed by the United States. It ended when Khomeini agreed to drink a jar of poison and sign a treaty with Saddam to end the war. In this war, millions of young men from both sides lost their lives. It was the duty of all young men to defend their countries, regardless of their religions or beliefs. It was their duty to fight and die for their homelands, yet Khomeini had reestablished an old law that discriminated against other religions. It was "if one member of a non-Muslim family converts to Islam, only he or she has the right to the entire family inheritance."

The new regime also encouraged families to have at least three or more children, in order to increase the Shiite Muslim population. The effect was a large, young population with no jobs, no freedom, and no future. There was an increase in the number of hopeless young criminals—addicts and drug dealers.

Imam Khomeini came with a vision and the idea to revise all the progress that Reza Shah and his son, Mohammed Reza Shah, had achieved. His policy was mostly to redirect the behavior of females under sharia law. Against his promise that he would continue as spiritual leader and reside in the holy city of Ghom, he became a dictator, occupied the shah's palace, and began to interfere with every aspect of citizens' lives.

For the Islamic Republic of Iran, the chador became a major headache. Modern young girls had no reason to follow the rules and hide their faces and hair under an ugly black cover. This reminded them of the worst time in the history of Persia, when women were taken by Arabs as sex slaves. It is shameful for a woman to hold this symbol of "Islamic hijab" as her value in society. It has been carved into a Muslim man's brain that a woman is a part of his belongings; therefore, he does not want to share her beauty with others. However, the chador is not protecting women, as it only raises curiosity and makes men more eager to discover what is hidden beneath. The chador has only benefited the sex trade; women are on every street corner in the cities. The chador is a cover to protect their identity and to prevent them from being bothered by a women's gestapo called the Sisters of Zainab. These sisters roam the streets in a pack of three to six to catch females who have colored their hair, have long, painted nails, or who do not wear proper Islamic hijabs. They punish them on the spot by cutting their hair with scissors and pulling their long nails with a plier. The hijab can only be black; other, more fashionable, clothing or colors are not acceptable.

Sadly, in the last thirty-five years of rule, the Islamic Republic in Iran has brought a lot of disappointment and misery to the lives of the people. Only the inner circle of a few top elite are doing very well. They not only receive their own share of oil money, but also they reach further and take the share of other citizens too. For that, they make sure the regime will survive. The outer circle, the majority, are the biggest losers. They used to be middle class; now they are poor or without a class. Catching up with 25 percent yearly inflation forces them to work two to three shifts daily. This gives them no time to complain. Some believe this special lifestyle has been programmed to keep them from protesting.

The younger generation blames the older for orchestrating the 1979 revolution. They miss freedom in every aspect of life. The government dictates and controls their lives. Sexual behavior, dress codes, and hijabs are the number one concerns of the regime, followed by unemployment, inflation, economy, and job creation. Recently, a mullah at a sermon opposing the shah's slogan—which was "Fewer children equals a better life"—insisted families should have up to fourteen children. He gave his blessing and promised his audience, "Heaven is your place if you go home tonight and make another child in the name of Ali and Zahra." Either he is ignorant or he has no knowledge of what is going on around him. He thinks the only responsibility of having a child is just to feed him and for that Allah is responsible. He repeated this expression "whoever gives them teeth will provide food too." Many of these children will grow up in poor families, with no education and grim futures. To survive, they choose the only option available to them— crime and drugs. They will end up in prison and in the end will be hanged in public places by the order of another mullah.

Iran is a rich country. Besides oil, it has been blessed with other natural resources and minerals. The people of Iran are poor because the contribution of that wealth is restricted to a few elite families. Most of the country's revenue stays in the mullahs' bank accounts in the form of dollars, euros, or other foreign currencies friendly with the regime. Every year, names of account holders with millions and billions in their names are published on the Internet; this caused the forbidding of the use of satellite dishes in Iran. They argue this is a sin that will send the men to hell by watching foreign women without hijab.

After the revolution, most of the population are government dependent and receive food stamps. Except a few who prosper, the rest have to work hard and hardly make ends meet. Many areas of the country are neglected; families live in cardboard sheds with no running water or electricity, dying from hunger and disease. Humans live worse than dogs, although dogs in Iran have a tough life too. The regime ignores this population as if it doesn't exist. Their priority is to raise the living standards and create prosperity for Shiites living in Lebanon, Iraq, Syria, and part of Africa. From time to time, you see on YouTube the glory and exceptional lifestyles of residents in northern Tehran as models of a modern Iran. The unique architectural designs of the beautiful, modern high-rises at the foot of Alborz Mountain, where the most expensive cars drive through boulevard highways to arrive. The residents have been immune to tough embargoes that have been imposed by the world on Iran for its nuclear reactor. This has made the world, especially Israel, nervous, as Iran cannot be trusted with a nuclear bomb. It is true, but the regime proved in the 2009 uprising of the Green Revolution that it will use any weapon, including the atomic bomb, to destroy the opposition. Therefore, Israeli Prime Minister Netanyahu should relax and let the people of Iran be worried.

While most Iranians have suffered under the embargo and waited for a better future, Iran's oil reserve is evaporating fast. Qatar in the south, under the Persian Gulf, and Iraq along the border with Iran are funneling oil out of Iran from underground reservoirs into heavy tankers while mullahs are busy fighting unruly females to keep them under the chador. They openly claim that all those bad things are happening in the world, and especially Iran, because of the women who are wearing improper Islamic hijab. Recently, a member of parliament mentioned another disaster; a new phenomenon called "stretch" has caused a headache for mullahs and lawmakers. It covers part of the body but is sexy and not compatible with Islamic hijab. The beautiful, intelligent Iranian women resist the order, especially in the hot summertime. They'd rather go to jail than wear the hijab.

Since the Islamic Republic of Iran is a religion-based government, any opposition to it is *mohareb ba khoda* (war against Allah). This means the suspect of a crime cannot be proven innocent in any court of law. The unusual but typical punishment for such a crime is that he or she will be handcuffed, blindfolded, and then taken to the rooftop of a high building. The doomed person will walk with a companion without knowledge of where he or she is. On the last step, he or she will be pushed to plummet to ground. This will be recorded to show on TV to be a lesson to disobedient young men and women.

During the shah's regime, human rights groups around the world had the key to any prison in Iran to make sure there was neither abuse nor political prisoners. The question is, where is the human rights watchdogs now? The worst human rights abuses are happening under this regime, and the world is looking away. Maybe to them, Iranians are not human anymore or they are humans without any rights.

An Iranian at any age is a politician, and the main topic in any gathering is politics. But when it comes to action, they are handicapped. They are like eunuchs; they know how, but they can't do anything. The conversation ends up with the final words, "If Britain or America are not in, it won't happen." For example, in the revolution of 1979, when Ramsey Clark, President Carter's envoy, met Khomeini in Paris, they sealed the fate of the shah and changed Iran and the world.

This has happened many times throughout Iranian history. In 2009 in Iran, a movement called the Green Movement of freedom-loving people tried to overthrow the tyrannical regime. The lives of hundreds of innocent men and women who longed for liberty and freedom were lost. Western countries looked the other way, either out of fear of the regime or because they believed it was not in their best interests to intervene. If the people of Iran had succeeded, the Middle East and the world would now be a better place to live.

Brain Drain

It was shortly after the revolution that the people of Iran started to leave and seek refuge in other countries. It was reported to Khomeini that the "brains" were leaving the country. His immediate response was, "Let them go; we don't need them."

There are only a few countries in the world that don't require visas for Iranians to enter. Among them are Malaysia, Indonesia, Turkey, and a few others. This has created the first step to exit Iran. Selling fake passports in those countries has become an established business. These can be bought freely everywhere—in shops or on the sidewalk. You have to choose the country of destination and then hand over your picture, and you are on the way to the airport. After boarding the airplane, destroy the fake passport. Upon arrival in the new country, claim refugee status. You will be provided with a lawyer, a hotel to stay in, and money to live on. With no criminal record or not having been part of the Iranian regime, you will be accepted. You can live, work, and enjoy freedom and life in the new country.

The reason that the people of Iran escape their country is because of the oppressive regime. It was not their intention to leave their motherland for so-called greener pastures. The story of the hardships and suffering in host countries they have gone to is the resonance of the revolution of 1979. Millions of citizens, especially the educated and intelligent, saw no future or hope for change and improvement in Iran. They risked the unknown and left the country they once loved so much.

In the presence of a different culture and language in the new country, they become a burden on the taxpayer. Many end up with a family break-up and divorce. In neighboring countries like Turkey, Pakistan, and countries around the Gulf that neither provide for refugees nor have any social support, young girls have to sell their bodies to support the family.

At first, most of the immigrants were hesitant to settle and start new lives elsewhere, because they thought the regime in Iran wouldn't last long. Years passed, and finally it became clear that this regime would continue to rule with force and an iron fist. It was time for refugees to seek a better, permanent place to make their new homes. Canada, the United States, and Australia were their first choices. Younger families started their own businesses. Lists of young, educated Iranians in high positions in the United States cover many pages on the Internet. Conservative and elder immigrants invested in safe, secure real estate. Many of them have experienced the boom and bust of real estate in their own countries before. They know in the long run that this will pay off.

Persian Holidays

The Islamic regime in Iran continues to root out and eliminate thousands of years of glorious Persian history and heritage in favor of tragedy and death that is associated with the barbaric acts of the Arabs on the land. They promote the Arabic language and religion at the expense of Persia. They are rewriting the history of Ali and his sons who murdered thousands of Persia's heroes and resistance fighters, and they are now making them out to be our heroes. The Islamic regime is trying to justify all the horrible acts from the Arabs on the land just because it was the only way to introduce Islam to Persia.

Kids from kindergarten are brainwashed about the grandeur of Islam and two of its heroes, Ali and Hussein. With time, the national holidays and traditional festivals and celebrations have been ignored and have been replaced with mourning and sad stories told

116

continually by mullahs to their audiences. The people hear stories about the black days of Persia when the Arabs took over the country and the religion and in exchange for which there is now the great religion of Islam.

The people of Iran have proven their intelligence throughout history, yet the Islamic regime with mullahs at the helm is trying to take them for a ride. This has backfired, and with any opportunity, the Iranians will rise and demand the lives they deserve to live in their beautiful land with its God-given bounty of natural resources. The more isolated the young and the future generation become from the free world and its progress, the more they become curious and ambitious to dig and shine the light to discover the truth about the past and to gain a sense of pride. At the risk of being arrested and punished, they continue to ignore the orders and do what other free nations do—be happy and live good lives, which is not a crime.

Iranians beyond the border, far from the harassment, continue to celebrate the rightful national holidays. Norooz (New Day) on March 21, the first day of spring and the beginning of the new year, is by far the largest national holiday. It has been celebrated for the past thousands of years. Zoroastrians in Iran continue to follow all traditional Persian holidays that have been deeply rooted in their beliefs and are all for happy occasions.

Conversion to Islam

The city of Yazd has been decorated with colorful lights, black flags, and the portrait of Ali crossing his legs and holding a sword across his knees. It is a day for celebration. A Zartoshti girl called Roshan is going to be converted to Islam and marry a young Muslim. She is only thirteen years old and has been missing for three days. This is an occasion that brings joy and excitement to the city that is otherwise a boring and quiet place. Jubilant drivers honk continually and congratulate each other. Some joyful citizens carry a tray of *noghl* (a round, white candy made of icing sugar) to offer to strangers and passers-by.

Now, only fifty thousand Zartoshti live in the country of birth of their prophet Zartosht, Iran, where for thousands of years the entire population had been Zartoshti. Their number is declining constantly, and soon they will be extinct. A Zartoshti must be born to the religion. Because this had been the only religion in Persia before Islam, one is not allowed to convert back from Islam to Zartoshti. On the contrary, if one member of a Zartoshti family converts to Islam, he or she will be the only beneficiary of the entire inheritance of that family. This law will override the will of the deceased. This is obviously not a conversion by convincing or through love and kindness.

Roshan's parents have been searching day and night for their daughter with the help of villagers. Finally, word comes that she is alive and well, living in a grand mullah's house in the nearby city of Yazd. Her father, a farm laborer, is pressing hard to stop the marriage, with the help of Zoroastrian elders. They meet the grand mullah at his house. Mullah himself opens the door, welcomes the guests, and offers them a seat on a wooden deck next to the pond at the center of the yard. After brief compliments from both sides, the mullah calls one of his wives to bring tea with pastry and cookies for the guests. He doesn't call her by her name, but uses an Arabic word for woman.

Minutes later, from one of the rooms, a woman wrapped in a black chador moves the curtain aside. She is holding a tray of tea in one hand through the chador, the other hand holding the lower part of her covering, and she holds the upper part with her teeth. With an acrobatic maneuver, she comes down three flights of stairs, leaves the tray on the table, and disappears again behind the curtain. Looking at her hand, one can determine she is white and fat.

Mullah manipulates the meeting; he does all the talking. He says, "It is true we are all Allah's creatures, but when the time comes and we stand in front of him, how can one ask for mercy, if one doesn't believe in him?" Then he quotes from the famous Persian poet Saadi, who said to Allah, "You, the creator and provider, if you care for your enemies like the gabr (fire worshippers) and tarsa (star worshippers), for sure you never ignore your friend, a Muslim."

Mullah went to madrasa to learn to read the Koran. From time to time, he cites verses of the Koran in Arabic with a fake Arabic accent and then translates them into Farsi for the guests. He enjoys criticizing the faith of others but imposes punishment on anyone who dares to criticize Islam or questions the Islamic religion. Usually for a minor remark, one can be forgiven by biting one's own tongue. Clearly, he has no tolerance for other religions. His plan is to convince the guests to join him and convert to Islam by explaining the advantages of being a Muslim in the society rather than a minority under pressure. He is convinced these people are in the dark and need to be guided with the light of Allah's messenger, Mohammad. He is gaining momentum and is sure he can soon ask the guests to join him and repeat the sacred words, "There is no other god than Allah, and

Mohammad is his messenger." The guests started to feel uncomfortable and are shifting in their seats.

When one of them interrupts the mullah and brings to his attention that they are here to release the young girl and let her go back to his family, the mullah angrily raises his voice and replies, "There is no return; she has already repeated the sacred words."

Before calling the meeting to an end, the mullah signals to Roshan's father to follow him for a private conversation. It doesn't take long before the father returns to his companions and asks them to join him and leave the place.

"Now what?" one of them asks him. The father is hesitant to answer but looks as if he is satisfied with the result. The mullah has convinced him that no Zartoshti man will now marry his daughter, especially after this incident. Besides, she is not such a beauty and from a poor family too. The mullah has promised him that he will find two other

123

Muslims suited to his two other elder daughters.

The mullah is short and fat. He had to look up to talk face-to-face with Roshan's father. A visible brown circle on his forehead shows he has paid his due to Allah by praying five times a day. This evidence is created from his forehead touching the ground in prayer. In the course of time, the act leaves this holy mark. For him, this has more value than any diploma on the wall. From his house and lifestyle, one could say he is rich and well established. Usually he makes his money by delivering sermons for occasions such as the commemoration of Imam Ali and his son Hussein, grievance for imams who died centuries ago.

He has done this many times before. He sits above the altar to deliver his sermon. He starts with some Arabic sentences and then continues with the same old story. He glamorizes the physique of Ali and Hussein and their images. As evidence, there is a portrait of Ali carrying a sword, with a beautiful face and green eyes, handsome like a Hollywood star. Then the mullah describes what good-hearted, caring, and loving persons they were. He continues to speak about their characters and bravery, telling how Ali beheaded nine opponents (Persian resistance fighters) in one movement.

Gradually, he moves into the mood of the drama. Lowering his head, he angrily tells the audience that Ayesha betrayed Ali and ordered men to brutally split his scalp in two with a poisoned saber. Then he continues with the drama of Hussein and his family who died in the hot desert of Karbala while begging for one drop of water. As the tragedy unfolds, men beat their foreheads with their palms and cry quietly. Women on the other side of the curtain beat their chests, pull their hair, and scream loudly. The mullah turns the volume up; the more tears he gets out of his audience, the more credit he gets for his act. All these acts originate from the time that Persia was under heavy pressure from caliphs; their stories show their anger and displeasure toward those caliphs.

.

Salman-e-Pars

In most books about Islam, Salman's name is mentioned. He was a Zoroastrian priest. Recently, in Iranian school books, he is praised for being the first Persian to accept Islam. Some other books celebrate him for helping Mohammad by teaching him the tricks and art of winning wars, particularly the famous war in Medina between him and his Quraysh tribe.

In that battle, Mohammad, with a small army, tricked the much larger army of the Quraysh. This brought him a sweet victory and raised his status. More importantly, this reopened the road for him to go back to Mecca where Mohammad was not allowed to go by the leader of his tribe.

It had been a common practice for Persian kings to choose their ministers from highly educated priests. Salman was one of the king's ministers. He was a certified *mobed-e-mobedan*

127

(priest of priests). He was a man with radical and revolutionary ideas and plans that were in opposition to the king's daily policy and governing. He was minister for some time until he lost his title and was dishonored. When his life was in danger, he fled his homeland with a broken heart, filled with hate and revenge toward the king.

The road to the west lay through the land of Arabia. He aimlessly followed merchant caravans, living with nomads and Bedouins. He used his knowledge and wisdom to help and win the hearts and souls of those desert dwellers by improving their daily lives, healing their wounds and sickness, and by teaching them how to prevent the spread of disease.

News about him spread fast through the caravans around the desert. His popularity grew among the poor, uneducated Arabs. When he arrived with the caravan that he was traveling with to Mecca, he was warmly welcomed by the leading Quraysh tribe. His arrival was celebrated, and all kinds of comforts were prepared for his stay. As he was tired from the constant traveling and moving from one location to another, he too was ready and happy to settle.

Salman never stopped spreading the seed of hate against the king and highlighting his weaknesses. Contrary to what Iranian schoolbooks say, he was not the first Persian to accept Islam; he vanished even before Mohammad declared his prophecy. To Zoroastrians, Salman is a traitor for his actions against Persia. In the end, he received the harsh punishment that he deserved. He was thrown alive into an abandoned well. His disappearance was noticed by the Quraysh's tribal leader, who started searching for him, dead or alive. At some point, they gave up the search, and it became an unsolved case. The truth was revealed when the perpetrator tried to cover up his crime by filling the well with dirt and rocks. When one asked, what is the purpose of doing this, the answer was, Satan (the devil) is at the bottom of this well. Since then, this has become a ritual act and obligation for pilgrims. When they are in Mecca for haj, they should travel to this site and throw a stone in this well.

The Spread of Islam in Modern Times

The Kingdom of Saudi Arabia and the Islamic Republic of Iran are in competition to expand their own brands of Islam around the world. Both have the means and money to do that. Saudis, who practice Sunni Islam, are focused mainly on the United States and Western Europe. They build mosques and Islamic centers in those countries. Some of these have become bases for so-called homegrown radicals. Since 9/11, the United States and Western countries are more resistant to the expansion of such facilities in their neighborhoods. The Iranian Islamic regime, with their missionaries like Hezbollah ("Army of Allah") is active in poor African countries and Shiite-dominant places, such as Lebanon and around the Gulf. They promote the Shiite branch with its own culture and traditions. The introduction of the commemoration of Hussein and his father, Ali, used to be just one of many Shiite practices; now it has become the core of their beliefs. A large percentage of Iran's oil revenue is spent in other Shiite countries, yet Sunnis don't consider Shiite Islam as a religion, because they don't follow the caliphs, the successors of the Prophet Mohammad. Sunnis and Shiites both live under sharia law. In Saudi Arabia, where people live under strict sharia law, a thief has to think twice before he steals, because if he is found guilty of the crime, his hand will be amputated.

Osama bin Laden was born in Saudi Arabia in a Sunni Muslim family. He chose to shortcut the Islamization of the world. He followed the path of Caliph Omar with the ultimate goal of spreading Islam by force and creating a world ruled by caliphs. Like Omar, he trained lowlife, hopeless young men, building an army of losers and suicidal men with the promise of a better life after death. They would go to the best part of paradise, with a stream of honey and lots of virgins, the things they were dreaming about on earth. He began to terrorize the greatest modern empire—the United States. He planned attacks against civilian and military targets in unpredictable places. He thought this would create fear in the hearts of people, followed by mayhem and panic, and that this would result in submission.

Osama continued his terrorist activities with no resistance and little consequence. He finally came to the conclusion that he too was dealing with a paper tiger. This encouraged him to commit his final act of 9/11. He thought this would bring the giant to its knees, and the rest of the world would follow. Osama did not succeed like Omar, because it was a different time with different leaders. He was aware that the fall of Persia at the hands of Omar was the force behind the existence and continuation of the religion of Islam. It nourished and grew with the blood of its victims until it became a religion beyond the Arabic-speaking world. A man will cut another human's head only after calling "Allah o Akbar." This encourages him to commit this act for the sake of Allah, and he considers himself a tool in Allah's hand.

This has caused an embarrassment to Allah. He is not happy to see his name dragged into such inhuman activity. Who knows how many times a day he has to apologize to other people's gods? Three-quarters of earth's population are non-Muslim; that makes them all Allah's enemy. Once, Allah, in a meeting with other gods, apologized for his followers' behaviors and asked them for a solution. The immediate response was that to correct the problem, he should get rid of heaven and its virgins altogether and send through his messenger a *sura* stating that bullying is bad and nothing to be proud of. Allah looked down and saw that thousands of his followers had blocked the streets and intersections to pray for him. This caused him embarrassment, and he was ashamed to see so much inconvenience to businesses, shopkeepers, drivers, and others, all because of him.

It is sad to see mullahs, the men of Allah, take advantage of their innocent believers and misguide them into hurting other humans. There is an expression—"Where the mullah has control over the intellect, it is difficult for a man's mind to work."

A widespread army of killing machines has been named after him, "hezb Allah" (party of Allah). Again, Allah not only denies being part of this, but also he strongly condemns it.

Allah, the god of Islam, and other gods have created men and women equally. Men should stop oppressing women and treating them like objects. Allah says he has nothing to do with sharia law. This law has been made by selfish men to maintain their superiority over their women.

At one point, Allah started to search his soul to see where he had made a mistake so that his believers had lost their direction and were not aligned with the rest of the world's nations. In the end, he came to the conclusion that his followers were not happy because they were neglected and placed in the worst part of the earth, where there is only sun and sand instead of waters and rivers. The only creature that does not complain there is the camel.

To correct the problem, he decided to place a lot of oil under their land and then he created the automobile. He thought this would make them rich and happy, enjoying living and minding their own business. Sadly, this didn't work either. On the contrary, this gave them more tools to make the world a miserable place for themselves and others. A terrorist always has reasons to justify his actions. Osama bin Laden was not happy to see the presence of infidels in the land of his prophet.

There is no justification to attack the United States, where more people are generous and giving to poor people around the world than anywhere else. If somewhere an earthquake, flood, or other natural disaster takes place, the world looks to America, because it has always been at the forefront of helping with its power and rescue facilities—no matter what country, what religion, or what people's color.

Billions of US dollars were spent in Africa to root out the AIDS disease. The whole world would suffer if the United States lost to terrorists. For Western countries, 9/11 was a warning and wake-up call. Osama's actions only worked against the efforts of world Islamization and of becoming ruled by caliphs. The tragedy and horror of 9/11 strengthened and united all nations, regardless of their ideology, party, or color. The day after 9/11, the national flag, the sign of patriotism, popped up in front of every building.

The non-radical Muslims feel their religion has been hijacked and that people now think of Islam as consisting mainly of radical Muslims. They cannot condemn the acts of terror because, from the very beginning, their religion has always been spread by force only.

Many Americans wrongfully believe they have done wrong in the past, and they are under the guilty impression that they deserve what the terrorists are doing to them and for that they are the target.

The irony is that Islam is the only religion that calls itself the religion of peace. From the beginning of its existence, it has been involved in war and destruction. Fourteen centuries later, suicide bombers kill themselves and many innocent people in their rush to get to paradise. The difference between a priest in a church and a mullah in a mosque is that the first one teaches to love your neighbor, to forgive his wrongdoings, and that we are all God's children, while the mullah calls for revenge, teaches hatred, and wants infidels to be hurt for being Allah's enemy.

Muslims are proud that their religion is spreading fast around the world and that one day the whole world will follow their religion. The question is, how much better would the world be then? What we see from the Muslim countries now is that as the world goes forward, they are going backward. They live in rich countries, but the people are poor. Peace is the name of their religion, but they are in constant war among themselves and with others. Islam has a quarter of the world's population and growing. They are aiming to be the number one religion on earth. While Jews are only 2 percent of the world's population, they have won a quarter of all Nobel Prize awards in science while Muslims have won only a handful.

After 9/11, the world, especially the United States, was not the same and will not be the same again. One of the Bin Laden's legacies is inconvenience at border crossings, long lineups, body searches, fingerprinting, and pictures taken. Those are now routine procedures for entering the country. After 9/11, Islam's name as the religion of peace has grown to several new names, such as "Muslim fanatics," "Muslim rebels," "Muslim militants," "Muslim fundamentalists," and "Muslim terrorists."

A new group of Muslims in the Middle East think they are the ultimate force to correct the world and set the direction of human life under the guidance of caliphs and sharia law. This new phenomenon is called ISIS, which stands for the Islamic State (of Iraq and Syria). If we include Iran with those two countries, this will be the creation of the caliphate as we knew it thirteen hundred years ago when caliphs ruled from Baghdad in Iraq over Syria, Iraq, and Iran.

ISIS is opposed to Shi'i Muslims, who have rejected caliphs as their leaders from the beginning of the creation of Islam. If ISIS is successful in Syria and Iraq, their next target would be Iran, where an unpopular regime continues to rule by force against the will of the majority of its citizens. The past harsh sanctions from the world on Iran have affected the military and defense systems, which are weak and out of date. The leaders are more interested in building an army of Shiite clergies around the world than in building a real army to defend the country against real enemies like ISIS.

Islam is like any other world religion. The only difference is that in Islam, religion and politics go hand in hand. In the name of religion, politicians misguide believers with all kinds of tricks, lies, and misinformation to brainwash them and make them into tools for their own plans and benefits.

When a man has been kept in the dark with little or no information, he is capable of acting like a robot. Attach a bomb to him, and let him kill himself and others. Turkey, a Muslim country, is a good example of a country where state and religion are two separate concepts and don't interfere with each other. The lawmaker has the freedom that is the foundation of democracy. The country is moving forward, side by side with other modern and civilized countries, in contrast to Iran, which is only going backward with mullahs at the helm.

Iranian mullahs use all the tools available to them to keep the population of Iran in the dark. The Iranian regime will only survive if it creates an atmosphere of trust and connects again with people as it did at the beginning of the revolution. Give people more freedom and do not interfere with their private lives. Happiness, laughter, and life enjoyment is everybody's right; don't make it a crime. A high percentage of Iranians are educated and are true believers of Shi'i Islam. For the last thirty-six years, the regime has pushed for the

Islamization of Iran with Islamic laws, which are not compatible with the Iranian mentality.

It was said that the generation after the revolution would grow up in an environment of pure Islamic rules and laws and then would become firm believers with higher standards and morals. Thereafter, the authorities would loosen their grips and leave the people so they could be role models to the rest of the world. As it is now, the pressure and control over the population has backfired. The regime has put itself in a corner and isolated itself from the rest of the world. To change course, mullahs should stay away from politics and let the experts establish democracy. Break free from non-practical Islamic rules. Join the rest of the world with civilized modern laws. Open the road for Iranians and make it easy for them to travel back and forth to their homeland. This will bring capitals with new ideas to build modern Iran for future generations.

Visiting the Homeland

The revolution of '79 brought Iran into the spotlight. The world did not know much about Iran, and it was seldom in the news. It was known that Iranians were rich and big spenders. They traveled the world with no visa requirements except for a few countries. The revolution of 1979 brought Iran into the spotlight all around the world as cameras focused on burning tires on the streets of Tehran. To the viewers, it seemed the whole world was on fire. The streets jammed with thousands of women wrapped in black Islamic hijabs, carrying plackets with pictures of Khomeini and shouting, "Death to Shah—Shah must go." The shah went, and with him, women's hard-earned freedom. And a woman value dropped to half of a man's.

Years after the revolution, I made plans to visit my homeland and for the first time to attend my father's gravesite.

I sent my old, expired passport to the Iranian Embassy and asked for new one. Soon after, I received my new passport with a stamp on the last page that explained that I could exit Iran within six months of the date of entry without paying the usual exit fee.

Mehrabad Airport in Tehran was not the same; it used to be an airport and a meeting place for young boys and girls to meet, have a drink, and listen to music. Now it was more like a holy place; pictures of the imam and other leaders covered the whole space.

At the counter, the customs officer checked my passport on a monitor. Instead of passing it back to me, he handed it to another man sitting behind him. The man signaled me to follow him to a room where he handed my passport to a young man at a desk and left. For a while, I thought nobody had noticed my presence. When he looked at my passport, he smiled and said, "I think we both are from the same city, Yazd."

After some friendly conversation, I thought he would hand me my passport and I would rush out to join friends and relatives who had come to receive me. He gave me good news. "You are free to go." When I asked for my passport, he replied, "You can pick it up at the passport office any time."

After hugging and kissing my friends and relatives, I apologized to them and explained my passport had been the cause of the delay. From their reaction, I got the feeling that it was more serious than I had thought. I have been traveling one and a half days to get there, and the time difference was nine and half hours. I was tired and couldn't sleep; I tossed in my bed or walked in my room the whole night. My mind was busy making plans of how to get out of Iran without a passport. I had seen the movie "Not without My Daughter." It gave me some hope. If a woman in a foreign country with a young child could go over the border, then it would be possible for me to do the same. I was innocent and had done nothing wrong in my life, but I had heard stories that here they killed first and then asked questions.

The revolution had long passed, but cleansing programs continue. It was a law to chase and find those who had served in the past shah's regime. They had to be jailed or executed. Every day in government-controlled newspapers, pages were filled with pictures of dead bodies of past politicians, activists, ministers, educators, and critics. Also a list of people labeled "forbidden to travel" had been posted to make sure that they could not obtain passports and should remain to pay the prices for their past activities. Many risked trying to escape the border through the mountains and passes without passports. They had been blacklisted "escapists," and the authorities were continually searching to find and punish them.

It was not clear to the government how and when I had left the country; with no record of my past I might be one of those escapists. The last time I left Iran was before the revolution. My file had been destroyed with other documents in the Canadian embassy before it had been closed. To avoid conflict with the Iranian regime regarding my dual citizenship, I left my Canadian passport in Canada. Now the burden was on my shoulders to prove that I had legally left Iran long before the revolution.

In the passport office in the section where passports could be picked up, in the row of *W* to *Z*, a young man behind the counter dressed as a Revolutionary Guard asked my last name. After a short search, he said my passport was not there. He listened to my short story of how I landed there. He showed me the chair behind me against the wall. A few minutes later, he jumped over the counter and signaled me to follow him. He walked fast along the courtyard to the opposite building. He climbed the stairs two at a time to the third floor. I followed him every step and arrived at a room where visitors were waiting, wall to wall, for only one clerk to handle their cases. My friend went straight to him and talked to his ear. It was a short, quiet conversation. On his way back to his desk, he told me I should be here the next day at 7:00 a.m., take the minibus with a carrier who would deliver my file and others like me to the Ministry of Justice.

The next day on arrival at the justice building, it was already packed with visitors. Some had become tired of standing, sat on the floor, and stretched their legs across the hallway. One had to step between their legs to get to the other side. There were all segments of people—young, old, children, women in black chadors, and some men handcuffed to prison guards. One of the men looked at me, put two fingers to his lip, and signaled to me, asking for a cigarette. I was sorry to say no. From the arrival to the end, I followed and watched the movement of my file with the passport from one room to the other. I asked the person who was carrying my file how long it usually takes to process this, and he replied two to three months. While I was sad and helpless, I saw an officer in a blue uniform from the old regime watching the crowd.

I walked over to him and casually told him my passport was there and my return ticket would expire in ten days; what were my options? He asked my name and for my file. He followed me, and I made sure he did not lose me in the crowd. He walked in the room and left the door ajar. While a clerk was registering the files in his book, my friend pulled out mine and put it on the top of others. Later, the man put my file under his arm and left the room. He walked fast, like a fish in an ocean of water among the crowd.

For fear of losing him in the crowd, I hung on to his jacket. He walked into a room filled with people and left my file on the desk in front of an unshaved man in plain clothing. I found an empty chair and waited. A few minutes passed, and then I discovered that this was a divorce court. The family of a groom and bride were fighting over alimony, and the man behind the desk was the judge. The court was in session, and he casually shoved other files in front of him while he was listening to arguments. When he touched my file, I stood up and indicated that was mine. He asked me to come forward and sit on an empty chair next to him. Occasionally, he asked me a simple question—where I lived, what I did, and so on—and I answered in short sentences while the court was in session and others in room continued arguing. He signed in the corner of the attachment and signaled the man who had brought me there, who stood on the side against the wall. I got up, thanked him, and then followed this man again. We went from one room to the next. At the end of the day, we arrived at a room marked "Boss." He knocked at the door, we entered, and he put the file in front of the boss and exited. The boss looked tired; the footsteps over the dust on his floor indicated he did not receive many visitors.

Without questioning me, he signed next to five other signatures and called the man who had brought in my file to take it. We arrived at the same room where first in the morning the passports were delivered. There the clerk told me they would send back my file to the passport office.

It was end of the day, and most of the visitors had left. I saw two of my morning companions waiting to be called. One of them had traveled twice with a fake passport; both times he had been arrested and sent back. The other tried to leave the country with a stolen passport. Now he wanted to ask the judge to forgive him so he could get a real passport.

The next day in the passport office, with the help of my friend, we found out that the day at the Ministry of Justice had been wasted time. Now, the file was with the office manager on the third floor of the same building. On the way there, he told me that if somebody asked me why he did this extra work for me, I should tell them I was his brother's friend. After arriving, he signaled me to stay outside, and he walked in. A few minutes later, he walked out without saying a word. He went straight to the stairs and back to his desk. A short time later, a fat, unshaven man walked out of his office straight toward me. I was the only one there; he came to me and said I should go to Ministry of Foreign Affairs to get a letter to indicate my past. I thanked him and rushed out to the street to catch a taxi. I had no idea where the ministry would be. The taxi driver told me it was in downtown Tehran near the bazaar. It was an old, three-story commercial building. To get into the building was similar to going to the United States at the airport. They searched bodies and gave you a number and a tray to empty your pockets. Here it was the same nightmare as at the Ministry of Justice. In a huge space, all the seats had been taken, and the rest of the people were standing against the wall, waiting to be called. Again, it was far from what I had expected.

Without hesitating, I went straight to the counter and told one of the clerks, "I am here to get a letter to indicate who I am and how I left the country." The clerk told me, "We don't have such information, and I can't help you."

I asked him to write this down on a piece of paper. He said no. I said, "Can you tell me your name?" He said, "You don't need it." When I insisted a voice in the background said, "You can tell them my name." I wrote down his name and rushed back to the passport office and straight to the manager. I knocked on his door, and he came out into the hallway. I told him the story. He didn't believe me; he knew this would take weeks not hours. I showed him the name of the person and asked him to call to confirm. He believed me but still could not make a decision. Here he had two options: either hand me the passport or leave it to authorities to judge my future. The outcome would be prison or worse.

To help him and make it easier for him, I began to tell him my background, religion, education, workplace and how, when, and why I'd left the country. He went back to his office, and a few minutes later, he told me I could pick up my passport the next day. The next day, I went to my friend to say good-bye. My friend jumped over the counter, hugged me, and handed me my passport, the item I had gone through hell to obtain.

One day before leaving the country, I walked through the neighborhood to take some pictures with my camcorder to show friends back in Canada. Suddenly, a young man jumped from the street over the narrow channel and grabbed my wrist, asking me to come with him to the police station. I resisted and pulled my hand back and asked why I should do that.

"Because we have to see what pictures you take," he replied. He was skinny and weak and shaking visibly. He had parked his car in traffic and left the door wide open. He asked my name, which I told him, and at the same time, I told him he could see the pictures there and then. When he insisted, I repeated, "I can show the pictures right now."

He looked at me and asked how. I rewound the film and asked him to look. After a few seconds he repeated my name, but wrongly, adding the word "fard" at the end. I believe he was testing my honesty. I corrected him, he released my hand and drove away.

I realized the magnitude of the event when I looked at the surrounding buildings where the occupants were jammed in the windows and watching. Similarly, the pedestrians and cars all wanted to see the end result. They were much surprised to see I was free to go. Now my concern was whether I should take my camcorder with me to the airport the next day. There at the customs counter, a young officer opened my suitcase, pulled out a silk carpet and stretched it over the counter. He acted as if he was appraising the carpet for export tax. With the corner of his mouth, he asked me how he could get to Canada. I answered his question; the step he would have to take was to get a visa.

He folded the carpet and put it back and said, "Have a good trip." I start to breathe again when airplane took off and I was in the air.

About the Author

The author was born in a village near the city of Yazd in Iran. He graduated from high school in Tehran in 1960. He received a master's degree in Mechanical Engineering from the University of Hannover, Germany. In 1970 he went back to Iran and worked there until 1974 when he emigrated to Canada.

Some stories in this book were passed on from generation to generation, and the rest were discovered by the author over the years.

When the birth of a religion begins with a human corpse being dragged by horses and left for hyenas and vultures to consume, fourteen centuries later, the world should not be surprised to see the cruel acts committed by terrorists in the name of Allah.

In this book, the author shines a light on the dark past of Persia under the rule of caliphs, imams, and mullahs. He argues that the world should be aware and recognize that ISIS (Islamic State) is a virus that ought to be taken seriously, and it should be stopped before it causes more harm to civilization.

53633410R00092

Made in the USA
Charleston, SC
14 March 2016